Verb
by

Paperback Edition

Published in New York, USA
February 2014

Thanks to Gloria for editing.

PLEASE DO NOT MAKE ILLEGAL COPIES OF THIS BOOK
COPYRIGHT © 2014 MICHAEL DIGIACOMO
ALL RIGHTS RESERVED
Any redistribution or reproduction of part or all of the contents in any form is prohibited. You may not, except with my express written permission, distribute or commercially exploit the content. Nor may you transmit it or store it on any other website or other form of electronic retrieval system.

ISBN: 978-0-9915079-1-7

A Message From Michael

Thank you for your interest in 225 American English Verb & Preposition Combinations.

My name is Michael DiGiacomo, and I am a native New Yorker. I have been helping language students learn English since the early 1990's. I began my formal language-teaching career in Sendai, Japan in 1994. Since then, I have worked in the ESL field as an instructor, a teacher trainer, an academic director, and a language school director. In 2004, I earned an MBA in Global Management. Now, I am the owner of Happy English, an English tutoring company in New York City. I teach students from all over the world here in New York, and online in their country.

I believe that language study should be both enjoyable and practical. In 2010 I started a website to provide a variety of English lessons to students all over the world. I set out to create lessons that were practical, easy to understand, and useful for self-study. Many of my students have given me ideas and suggestions for lessons and this book grew out of some of those ideas.

You can find my website at **www.myhappyenglish.com**

Prepositions are troublesome for a lot of English language students. While there are many uses of prepositions in English, this book focuses on verb and preposition combinations. Unlike phrasal verbs, which have an idiomatic usage, the verb and preposition combinations presented here in this book are collocations. This means that they are, as I like to call them, just "set phrases."

For example, the verb **listen** generally takes the preposition **to**, as in "I like to **listen to** jazz." I have put together a collection of 225 of the most common verb and preposition combinations I could find. I hope you find this book helpful for studying them!

As always, thanks for studying with me.

Table of Contents

A Message From Michael 2
Table of Contents 4
Key Points About Prepositions 14
Focus On The Meaning Of Prepositions 16
No. 1: account for 24
No. 2: accuse of 24
No. 3: adapt to 25
No. 4: add to 25
No. 5: adjust to 26
No. 6: admire for 26
No. 7: admit to 27
No. 8: agree on 27
No. 9: agree with 28
No. 10: apologize for 28
No. 11: apologize to 29
No. 12: apply for 29
Review Quiz #1 30
No. 13: apply to 32
No. 14: approve of 32
No. 15: argue about 33
No. 16: argue with 33
No. 17: arrange for 34
No. 18: ask about 34
No. 19: ask for 35
No. 20: base on 35
No. 21: become of 36

No. 22: beg for 36
No. 23: begin with 37
No. 24: believe in 37
Review Quiz #2 38
No. 25: belong to 40
No. 26: benefit from 40
No. 27: blame for 41
No. 28: boast about 41
No. 29: borrow from 42
No. 30: care about 42
No. 31: care for 43
No. 32: charge with 43
No. 33: choose between 44
No. 34: collide with 44
No. 35: come from 45
No. 36: comment on 45
Review Quiz #3 46
No. 37: communicate about 48
No. 38: communicate with 48
No. 39: compare to 49
No. 40: compare with 49
No. 41: compete in 50
No. 42: compete with 50
No. 43: complain about 51
No. 44: complain to 51
No. 45: compliment on 52
No. 46: concentrate on 52

No. 47: confess to 53
No. 48: confuse with 53
Review Quiz #4 54
No. 49: congratulate for 56
No. 50: congratulate on 56
No. 51: consent to 57
No. 52: consist of 57
No. 53: contribute to 58
No. 54: convince of 58
No. 55: cope with 59
No. 56: correspond with 59
No. 57: cover with 60
No. 58: crash into 60
No. 59: cure of 61
No. 60: decide against 61
Review Quiz #5 62
No. 61: decide between 64
No. 62: decide on 64
No. 63: demand from 65
No. 64: depend on/for 65
No. 65: derive from 66
No. 66: deter from 66
No. 67: devote to 67
No. 68: differ from 67
No. 69: disagree with 68
No. 70: disapprove of 68
No. 71: discourage from 69

No. 72: discuss with 69
Review Quiz #6 70
No. 73: distinguish from 72
No. 74: distract from 72
No. 75: dream about 73
No. 76: dream of 73
No. 77: dress in (1) 74
No. 78: dress in (2) 74
No. 79: drink to 75
No. 80: elaborate on 75
No. 81: emerge from 76
No. 82: escape from 76
No. 83: exchange for 77
No. 84: exclude from 77
Review Quiz #7 78
No. 85: excuse for 80
No. 86: excuse from 80
No. 87: expel from 81
No. 88: experiment on 81
No. 89: experiment with 82
No. 90: explain to 82
No. 91: face with 83
No. 92: feel about 83
No. 93: feel for 84
No. 94: fight against 84
No. 95: fight for 85
No. 96: fight with 85

Review Quiz #8 86
No. 97: forget about 88
No. 98: forgive for 88
No. 99: get married to 89
No. 100: graduate from 89
No. 101: grumble about 90
No. 102: guess at 90
No. 103: happen to 91
No. 104: hear about 91
No. 105: hear from 92
No. 106: hear of 92
No. 107: help with 93
No. 108: hide from 93
Review Quiz #9 94
No. 109: hinder from 96
No. 110: hope for 96
No. 111: impress on 97
No. 112: insist on 97
No. 113: insure against 98
No. 114: interfere in 98
No. 115: interfere with 99
No. 116: introduce to 99
No. 117: invest in 100
No. 118: invite for 100
No. 119: invite to 101
No. 120: involve in 101
Review Quiz #10 102

Special Bonus Lesson: Prepositions With Made 104
No. 121: joke about 106
No. 122: joke with 106
No. 123: keep for 107
No. 124: keep away from 107
No. 125: know about 108
No. 126: laugh about 108
No. 127: laugh at 109
No. 128: learn about 109
No. 129: leave for 110
No. 130: leave from 110
No. 131: lend to 111
No. 132: listen for 111
Review Quiz #11 112
No. 133: listen to 114
No. 134: long for 114
No. 135: look at 115
No. 136: look for 115
No. 137: matter to 116
No. 138: meet with 116
No. 139: mistake for 117
No. 140: object to 117
No. 141: operate with 118
No. 142: participate in 118
No. 143: pay for 119
No. 144: persist in 119
Review Quiz #12 120

No. 145: plan on	122
No. 146: praise for	122
No. 147: pray for	123
No. 148: pray to	123
No. 149: prefer to	124
No. 150: prepare for	124
No. 151: present with	125
No. 152: prevent from	125
No. 153: prohibit from	126
No. 154: protect from	126
No. 155: provide for	127
No. 156: provide with	127
Review Quiz #13	128
No. 157: punish for	130
No. 158: quarrel about	130
No. 159: quarrel with	131
No. 160: react to	131
No. 161: recover from	132
No. 162: refer to	132
No. 163: relate to	133
No. 164: rely on	133
No. 165: remind about	134
No. 166: remind of	134
No. 167: reply to	135
No. 168: rescue from	135
Review Quiz #14	136
No. 169: resign from	138

No. 170: respond to 138

No. 171: result in 139

No. 172: retire from 139

No. 173: return from 140

No. 174: rob of 140

No. 175: save from 141

No. 176: scold for 141

No. 177: search for 142

No. 178: see about 142

No. 179: see to 143

No. 180: send for 143

Review Quiz #15 144

No. 181: separate from 146

No. 182: share with 146

No. 183: shout at 147

No. 184: show up at 147

No. 185: smile at 148

No. 186: speak to 148

No. 187: speak about 149

No. 188: specialize in 149

No. 189: spend on 150

No. 190: stand for 150

No. 191: stare at 151

No. 192: stem from 151

Review Quiz #16 152

No. 193: stop from 154

No. 194: subject to 154

No. 195: subscribe to 155
No. 196: substitute for 155
No. 197: subtract from 156
No. 198: succeed at 156
No. 199: succeed in 157
No. 200: suffer from 157
No. 201: suspect of 158
No. 202: talk about 158
No. 203: talk to 159
No. 204: talk with 159
Review Quiz #17 160
No. 205: tell about 162
No. 206: thank for 162
No. 207: think about 163
No. 208: think of 163
No. 209: translate from/into 164
No. 210: travel to 164
No. 211: turn to 165
No. 212: use for 165
No. 213: vote for 166
No. 214: vouch for 166
No. 215: wait for 167
No. 216: walk into 167
Review Quiz #18 168
No. 217: warn about 170
No. 218: warn against 170
No. 219: waste on 171

12

No. 220: wish for 171

No. 221: wonder about 172

No. 222: work for 172

No. 223: work in 173

No. 224: work on 173

No. 225: work with 174

No. 226: worry about 174

No. 227: write about 175

No. 228: write to 175

Review Quiz #19 176

Quiz Answer Key 178

Index Reference 179

Other paperbacks & eBooks by Michael DiGiacomo 186

Key Points About Prepositions

A preposition is a word which comes before a noun or a pronoun and shows the relationship between that noun or pronoun and other words in the sentence. Here are some examples of prepositions:
- This is the charger **for** my cell phone. *The preposition **for** shows the relationship between the charger and the cell phone.*
- Jack works **with** his brother. *The preposition **with** shows the relationship between Jack and his brother.*

Some prepositions are used to show the location of a noun or pronoun:
- The dog is sleeping **on** the sofa. *The preposition **on** shows the location of the dog.*
- There is a pen **near** the book. *The preposition **near** shows the location of the book.*

Other prepositions are used to show time and directional relationships:
- I took a nap **after** lunch. *The preposition **after** relates to the time of the nap.*
- Jack took a train **to** Manhattan. *The preposition **to** shows the direction of the train.*

Note also that **to** is used in the infinitive form (to + verb) of the verb. Many verbs are followed by an infinitive form, and as such those have not been included in this book:
- I like **to eat** pizza.
- We want **to see** a movie tomorrow.

In many cases, prepositions pair with verbs and adjectives as collocations. In this book, I am going to focus on 225 of these combinations of verbs and prepositions. I am also going show you some informational columns where we will look at the prepositions themselves, what they mean and how they are used.

These preposition and verb combinations need to be memorized. I hope this book, and the lessons in it help you do that.

Ready? Let's get started!

Focus On The Meaning Of Prepositions

About

About introduces a topic. **About** is followed by the noun which is the topic of the action of the verb:

- We talked **about** the party. *The topic of talking was the party.*

- Jack complained **about** the food to the waiter. *The topic of complaining was the food.*

- How do you feel **about** the company's decision to move to Chicago? *The topic of feeling was the company's decision.*

Against

Against introduces the opposition of or resistance to something. **Against** is followed by a noun which shows the opposition action of the verb and the opposition of the subject:

- Many people voted **against** the tax increase. *The people opposed the tax increase.*

- ABC Company is fighting **against** several competitors. *ABC Company is fighting in opposition to several competitors.*

- We were warned **against** going to that part of the town. *We were warned in opposition to going to that part of the town.*

At

At introduces a certain or particular point. **At** is followed by a noun which is the target point of the action of the verb:

- I looked **at** Jane and smiled. *Jane is the target point of my looking.*

- The children were pointing **at** the clowns when they marched in the parade. *The clowns were the target point of the children's pointing.*

- The train showed up **at** the station late. *The station is the target point of the action of the train's showing up.*

Between

Between shows a connecting relationship involving two nouns. **Between** is followed by a noun which has a connecting relationship to another noun both of which receive the action of the verb:

- We can choose **between** chocolate and vanilla ice cream. *Chocolate and vanilla ice cream are connected to the action of choosing.*

- We need to decide **between** New York and Boston for the meeting. *New York and Boston are the two places that are connected to the act of deciding.*

For

For introduces a person or thing receiving some benefit or support of the verb:

- I baked this cake **for** your birthday! *Your birthday received the benefit of my baking.*

- I think I will vote **for** Jim to be the class president. *Jim will receive the benefit of my voting.*

For also introduces the place which is the destination of the subject of the verb:

- Brad is leaving **for** Mexico City tomorrow. *Mexico City is the destination Brad will travel to.*

For also introduces the noun which has a relationship with the subject and with regard to the action of the verb:

- I've been working **for** this company for three years. *This company is the place where I work.*

- I'm longing **for** a dish of chocolate ice cream. *A dish of chocolate ice cream is the object of my longing.*

For also introduces the purpose and/or function of the action of the verb:

- I'm looking **for** a new apartment. *A new apartment is the purpose of looking.*

- I want to apologize **for** being late. *Being late is the purpose of apologizing.*

From

From shows the origin point in space or time where something begins or starts:

- They came **from** our main office in Chicago. *Our main office in Chicago is the origin point of their coming.*

- The workshop is **from** Monday to Thursday. *Monday is the starting point of the workshop.*

From shows the source or origin of someone or something

- Megumi is **from** Japan. *Japan is Megumi's origin.*

- These cookies came **from** Tracker Jim's grocery store. *Tracker Jim's is the source of the cookies.*

In

In is used to indicate a person's occupational field or business:

- Hayato works **in** the banking industry. *The banking industry is the field in which Hayato is employed.*

- Tim quit his job **in** sales and started his own business. *Sales is the field in which Tim was employed.*

In is also used to show the object or situation of inclusion or participation:

- We were involved **in** the planning meeting. *The planning meeting was the situation in which we participated.*

- I never invest **in** risky stocks. *Risky stocks are the objects in which I do not invest.*

In is also used to indicate the situation where something is enclosed and/or surrounded by something:

- The girl was dressed **in** a pink dress. *A pink dress is the object surrounding the girl.*

- Jenny is standing **in** the room. *The room is the thing that is surrounding Jenny.*

Into

Into introduces the object of the result of physical contact:

- A car crashed **into** a telephone pole today. *A telephone pole was the point of physical contact of the car.*

- Danny said he walked **into** a door because he wasn't paying attention. *A door was the point of physical contact of Danny.*

Into also shows a transformation from one form of something to another form:

- His book has been translated **into** several languages. *Several languages are the result of the transformation of translating.*

- Clark Kent turned **into** Superman and saved the city. *Superman is the result of Clark Kent's transformation.*

Of

Of is used to show the relationship between a verb that shows a mental state and its object:

- I think **of** you every day. *You are the object in my thinking.*

- We know **of** many good restaurants in NYC. *Many good restaurants in NYC are the objects of our knowledge.*

Of is also used to show the relationship between verbs of change and their objects:

- Nothing became **of** the meeting we had about marketing. *The meeting we had about marketing didn't change anything.*

- That medicine cured Rob **of** his cold. *That medicine changed Rob's medical condition.*

Of is also used to express a cause or reason for some action:

- He accused me **of** taking his iPod. *Taking his iPod is the cause of his accusing.*

- I convinced him **of** stopping smoking. *Stopping smoking is the reason for my convincing.*

Of is also used to show the material or contents that something is created with:

- This book consists **of** 225 verb and preposition combinations. *225 verb and preposition combinations are contained in this book.*

On is used to show the relationship the object has to the verb. The object is the target of the action of the verb:

- You can always depend **on** the trains in this town to run on time. *The trains are the targets of depending.*

- Can you elaborate **on** your last point? *Your last point is the target of elaborating.*

- We all agree **on** Jack's plan. *Jack's plan is the target of our agreeing.*

To

To is used to show movement in the direction of a place, or the intended location, or the point of reference of the action of the verb:
- I drove **to** the office. *The office is the intended location of driving.*

- If you walk **to** the train station and turn left, you'll see the café. *The direction of the train station is the point of reference of walking.*

To is also used when we show the person or people who are the recipient or potential recipient of something. This something could be a physical object or an abstract idea:
- Jack gave flowers **to** his girlfriend. *His girlfriend is the recipient of Jack's giving.*

- People should be kind **to** animals. *Animals are the potential recipients of the abstract idea of kindness.*

With

With shows something or someone is acting, doing, or moving in the same direction or time as another thing or person:
- I usually agree **with** my boss. *My boss and I usually agree.*

- This memo corresponds **with** the information presented at the meeting. *This memo and the information presented at the meeting correspond.*

In a similar way, **with** can show two things in opposition:
- I disagree **with** her. *Her and I are in opposition.*

- The music interferes **with** my studying. *My studying and the music are in opposition.*

With also describes the material use as clothing or covering:

- The glasses are covered **with** a towel. *A towel is the material used for covering the glasses.*

- Jen is dressed **with** the finest outfit she could find. *The finest outfit she could find is the material used as clothing.*

No. 1: account for

Grammar Pattern:
- **account for** [something]

Preposition Focus:
- We use **for** to indicate the purpose of accounting.

Usage:
- A person can **account for** money, or other valuable items such as the inventory of a store or warehouse.

Examples:
- We need to **account for** all of the money.
- The boss said that after the trade show, we were unable to **account for** all of the laptops.

No. 2: accuse of

Grammar Pattern:
- **accuse** [someone] **of**

Preposition Focus:
- We use **of** to show the reason of accusing.

Usage:
- A person can **accuse** another person **of** doing something wrong.

Examples:
- The boss **accused** Bob **of** missing the deadline

- I can't believe that Danny **accused** me **of** being rude in the meeting. I was just trying to answer his question.

No. 3: adapt to

Grammar Pattern:
- **adapt** to [something]

Preposition Focus:
- We use **to** when we show the object of adapting.

Usage:
- A person can **adapt to** a new job, a new home, or a new living place.

Examples:
- We can **adapt** this software **to** any environment.

- I'm looking forward to my new assignment in New York. I think I can easily **adapt to** living there.

No. 4: add to

Grammar Pattern:
- **add** [something] **to** [something]

Preposition Focus:
- We use **to** when we show the object of adding.

Usage:
- A person can **add** something **to** another thing.

Examples:
- The chef **added** chili **to** the curry.

- **Adding** this modification **to** the software will add two weeks to the project.

No. 5: adjust to

Grammar Pattern:
- **adjust to** [something]

Preposition Focus:
- We use **to** when we show the object of adjusting.

Usage:
- A person can **adjust to** a new job, a new home, or a new living place.

Examples:
- Chris finally **adjusted to** life in New York.

- I think it is not going to be easy for everyone to **adjust to** this new work schedule.

No. 6: admire for

Grammar Pattern:
- **admire** [someone] **for**

Preposition Focus:
- We use **for** to indicate the purpose of admiring.

Usage:
- A person can **admire** another person **for** their achievement, or their special ability. Children often admire their parents and/or heroes.

Examples:
- I **admire** my grandfather **for** his hard work.

- Everyone **admires** David **for** his talent.

No. 7: admit to

Grammar Pattern:
- **admit** [something] **to** [something]

Preposition Focus:
- We use **to** when we show the object of admitting.

Usage:
- A person can **admit to** making a mistake, or failing to do something.

Examples:
- Doug **admitted** his mistake **to** the boss.
- I **admitted** that I was wrong **to** Jane. I think she can forgive me.

No. 8: agree on

Grammar Pattern:
- **agree on** [something]

Preposition Focus:
- We use **on** to show the target of agreeing.

Usage:
- A person can **agree on** an idea, a proposal a time schedule, etc.

Examples:
- We can not **agree on** this contract unless you change the terms.

- I **agreed on** some of the proposed changes in the plan, but not all of them.

No. 9: agree with

Grammar Pattern:
- **agree with** [someone]

Preposition Focus:
- We use **with** to show the object of agreeing.

Usage:
- A person can **agree with** another person.

Examples:
- I don't **agree with** Jim.
- It's not easy to **agree with** the new manager.

No. 10: apologize for

Grammar Pattern:
- **apologize for** [something]

Preposition Focus:
- We use **for** to indicate the purpose of apologizing.

Usage:
- A person can **apologize for** forgetting something, breaking something, or any other behavior that disturbs other people.

Examples:
- I **apologized for** the mistake.
- You should **apologize for** missing the meeting. The boss is pretty upset about it.

No. 11: apologize to

Grammar Pattern:
- **apologize to** [someone]

Preposition Focus:
- We use **to** when we show the object of apologizing.

Usage:
- A person can **apologize to** another person.

Examples:
- I have to **apologize to** the boss for the trouble.

- I **apologized to** my wife, but she is still angry with me.

No. 12: apply for

Grammar Pattern:
- **apply for** [something]

Preposition Focus:
- We use **for** to indicate the purpose of applying.

Usage:
- A person can **apply for** a driver license, a bank loan, a job, etc.

Examples:
- I am going to **apply for** a truck driver's license.

- We need to **apply for** a construction permit before we begin the work.

Review Quiz #1

Read the sentence and choose the correct preposition (a, b, c, or d) that correctly completes the sentence.

1. The auditor said we need to account _____ all of the postage stamps
    a. for   b. of   c. in   d. with

2. When I accused her _____ making a mistake she got angry.
    a. for   b. of   c. by   d. to

3. He's flexible and can adapt _____ any situation.
    a. about   b. of   c. to   d. with

4. I added two slides _____ the presentation. I think it's finished now.
    a. to   b. in   c. for   d. on

5. I couldn't adjust _____ working with my boss for a long time.
    a. of   b. to   c. about   d. for

6. I admire her _____ her ability to work and go to school.
    a. from   b. on   c. against   d. for

7. You should admit _____ the manager that you made a mistake.
    a. with   b. at   c. into   d. to

8. It will be difficult for everyone to agree _____ this contract.
    a. away   b. on   c. if   d. upon

9. I understand what you are saying, but I don't agree _____ you.
    a. with   b. between   c. to   d. in

30

10. I tried to apologize_____ what I said but she was so angry she didn't answer my call.
    a. for　　　b. of　　　c. in　　　d. to

11. I apologized _____ the boss and explained what happened.
    a. at　　　b. to　　　c. for　　　d. by

12. It's a pain in the neck to apply _____ a driver's license.
    a. with　　　b. about　　　c. of　　　d. for

No. 13: apply to

Grammar Pattern:
- **apply to** [a school]

Preposition Focus:
- We use **to** when we show the object of applying.

Usage:
- A person can **apply to** a private high school, a college, or a university.

Examples:
- Jane's son has **applied to** several Universities in New York City.
- I **applied to** Harvard, Princeton, and Yale.

No. 14: approve of

Grammar Pattern:
- **approve of** [something]

Preposition Focus:
- We use **of** to show the object of approving.

Usage:
- A person can **approve of** an idea, a proposal, or even another person's behavior.

Examples:
- I do not **approve of** smoking in this office.
- The company does not **approve of** us wearing jeans to the office

No. 15: argue about

Grammar Pattern:
- **argue about** [something]

Preposition Focus:
- We use **about** to indicate the topic of arguing.

Usage:
- People can **argue about** a topic.

Examples:
- They usually **argue about** money.

- You should never **argue about** anything with a customer.

No. 16: argue with

Grammar Pattern:
- **argue with** [someone]

Preposition Focus:
- We use **with** to show the object of arguing.

Usage:
- A person can **argue with** another person.

Examples:
- Jack has been **arguing with** his wife recently.

- Why is Ethan **arguing with** the boss? What happened?

No. 17: arrange for

Grammar Pattern:
- **arrange for** [something]

Preposition Focus:
- We use **for** to indicate the purpose of arranging.

Usage:
- A person can **arrange for** a situation, like a meeting, or transportation, lodging, etc.

Examples:
- We **arranged for** a car and a driver to meet the CEO at the airport.

- The travel department **arranged** hotel rooms **for** everyone attending the trade show.

No. 18: ask about

Grammar Pattern:
- **ask** [someone] **about** [someone/topic]

Preposition Focus:
- We use **about** to indicate the topic of asking.

Usage:
- A person can **ask about** a topic, an issue, or another person.

Examples:
- I **asked** Greg **about** the meeting.

- I tried to **ask** Eddie **about** the meeting schedule, but he isn't in his office today.

No. 19: ask for

Grammar Pattern:
- **ask** [someone] **for** [something]

Preposition Focus:
- We use **for** to indicate the purpose of asking.

Usage:
- A person can **ask** another person **for** something.

Examples:
- You can **ask** me **for** anything. I am happy to help.

- If you **ask** the receptionist **for** a pamphlet I am sure she can get one for you.

No. 20: base on

Grammar Pattern:
- **base** [something] **on** [something]

Preposition Focus:
- We use **on** to show the target of basing.

Usage:
- Something is **based on** ingredients or components.

Examples:
- We **based** the HR policy **on** the manager's suggestions.

- We **based** this budget **on** next quarter's sales projections.

No. 21: become of

Grammar Pattern:
- **become of** [someone]/[something]

Preposition Focus:
- We use **of** to show the object of becoming.

Usage:
- A situation can **become of** a person or a thing.

Examples:
- I think nothing good will **become of** the sales leads I received from Joe.

- Nothing **became of** the discussion we had about changing the vacation policy.

No. 22: beg for

Grammar Pattern:
- **beg** [someone] **for** [something]

Preposition Focus:
- We use **for** to indicate the purpose of begging.

Usage:
- A person can **beg** someone **for** something.

Examples:
- A guy in the train station **begged** us **for** money.

- I had to **beg** the boss **for** a day off because I had a dentist appointment.

No. 23: begin with

Grammar Pattern:
- **begin with** [something]

Preposition Focus:
- We use **with** to show the object of beginning.

Usage:
- A situation or event can **begin with** something.

Examples:
- Let's **begin** the meeting **with** a speech by the chairman.

- I always **begin** the work day **with** a quick staff meeting.

No. 24: believe in

Grammar Pattern:
- **believe in** [something]

Preposition Focus:
- We use **in** to show the object of believing.

Usage:
- A person can **believe in** something.

Examples:
- The CEO doesn't **believe in** employees working on the weekend.

- My father **believed in** working hard and saving money.

Review Quiz #2

Read the sentence and choose the correct preposition (a, b, c, or d) that correctly completes the sentence.

1. Jim applied _____ a prestigious high school for his son.
    - a. to
    - b. in
    - c. for
    - d. on

2. My wife doesn't approve _____ me going to the bar with my friends.
    - a. about
    - b. to
    - c. for
    - d. of

3. My neighbors always argue _____ everything.
    - a. on
    - b. about
    - c. against
    - d. from

4. I argued _____ her all night last night.
    - a. to
    - b. at
    - c. into
    - d. with

5. I arranged _____ coffee and tea to be served during the meeting.
    - a. upon
    - b. if
    - c. away
    - d. for

6. I need to ask you _____ something. Are you busy now?
    - a. about
    - b. with
    - c. between
    - d. in

7. I think we should ask the customer _____ their opinion on this proposal.
    - a. in
    - b. of
    - c. for
    - d. with

8. This invoice is based _____ work done since June 3rd.
    - a. for
    - b. by
    - c. on
    - d. to

9. I hope something becomes _____ what we talked about in the meeting.
    - a. about
    - b. for
    - c. of
    - d. with

10. She's busy, but I begged her _____ the chance to have a meeting next week.
    a. for   b. in   c. of   d. on

11. The boss began his speech _____ a summary of last month's sales.
    a. of   b. about   c. with   d. for

12. Do you believe _____ ghosts?
    a. from   b. in   c. against   d. on

No. 25: belong to

Grammar Pattern:
- **belong to** [someone]

Preposition Focus:
- We use **to** when we show the object of belonging.

Usage:
- Something **belongs to** a person.

Examples:
- These files **belong to** the HR department.

- I **belong to** the marketing department of my company.

No. 26: benefit from

Grammar Pattern:
- **benefit from** [something]

Preposition Focus:
- We use **from** to indicate the source of benefiting.

Usage:
- A person or organization can **benefit from** something.

Examples:
- I think we can **benefit from** the training program.

- If you can give a presentation on motivation at the meeting, I think everyone will **benefit from** it.

No. 27: blame for

Grammar Pattern:
- **blame** [someone/something] **for** [something]

Preposition Focus:
- We use **for** to indicate the purpose of blaming.

Usage:
- A person can **blame** something or someone **for** something.

Examples:
- The boss **blamed** Hank **for** the drop in sales.

- The economic downturn of 2009 was **blamed for** the drop in sales.

No. 28: boast about

Grammar Pattern:
- **boast about** [something]

Preposition Focus:
- We use **about** to indicate the topic of boasting.

Usage:
- A person can **boast about** something.

Examples:
- Jack was **boasting about** his promotion.

- If you continue **boasting about** your good fortune, people will not want to talk to you.

No. 29: borrow from

Grammar Pattern:
- **borrow** [something] **from** [someone]

Preposition Focus:
- We use **from** to indicate the source of borrowing.

Usage:
- A person can **borrow** something **from** a person or place.

Examples:
- We need to **borrow** a projector **from** the IT department for the trade show.
- I had to **borrow** some money **from** Dianne today.

No. 30: care about

Grammar Pattern:
- **care about** [someone]/[something]

Preposition Focus:
- We use **about** to indicate the topic of caring.

Usage:
- A person can **care about** another person or a thing.

Examples:
- The manager really **cares about** employee benefits.

- I don't **care about** my staff coming a little late to work, as long as they finish their work.

No. 31: care for

Grammar Pattern:
- **care for** [someone]/[something]

Preposition Focus:
- We use **for** to indicate the purpose of caring.

Usage:
- A person can **care for** another person.

Examples:
- I don't **care for** the new salesman. He's a bit conceited.

- I don't **care for** the painting they put up in the reception area. Do you think we can change it?

No. 32: charge with

Grammar Pattern:
- **charge** [someone] **with**

Preposition Focus:
- We use **with** to show the object of charging.

Usage:
- A person can be **charged with** a task or a project.

Examples:
- I have been **charged with** revising the company website.

- Bob is an expert, so I decided to **charge** him **with** setting up the marketing plan for next year.

No. 33: choose between

Grammar Pattern:
- **choose between** [A] and [B]

Preposition Focus:
- We use **between** to indicate two things connected to choosing.

Usage:
- A person can **choose between** two things.

Examples:
- We need to **choose between** Joe and Tom for the job.
- You can **choose between** tea or coffe with lunch.

No. 34: collide with

Grammar Pattern:
- **collide with** [someone]/[something]

Preposition Focus:
- We use **with** to show the object of colliding.

Usage:
- A person or an object can **collide with** another person or object.

Examples:
- I almost **collided with** the receptionist when I entered the lobby.
- I heard an asteroid **collided with** the moon.

No. 35: come from

Grammar Pattern:
- **come from** [somewhere]

Preposition Focus:
- We use **from** to indicate the original place.

Usage:
- A person or object can **come from** a place.

Examples:
- The marketing manager **came from** our main office in Chicago.
- This server **came from** our branch office in Boston.

No. 36: comment on

Grammar Pattern:
- **comment on** [something]

Preposition Focus:
- We use **on** to show the target of commenting.

Usage:
- A person can **comment on** something.

Examples:
- The boss **commented** favorably **on** my report.
- I am going to **comment on** the new HR policy during the staff meeting tomorrow.

Review Quiz #3

Read the sentence and choose the correct preposition (a, b, c, or d) that correctly completes the sentence.

1. Who does this tablet belong _____?
   a. for   b. to   c. at   d. into

2. I think we can all benefit _____ a long vacation at the end **of** the year.
   a. away   b. from   c. if   d. upon

3. We can't blame Greg _____ what happened.
   a. for   b. in   c. with   d. from

4. Stop boasting _____ your winning lottery ticket. It was just $50.
   a. about   b. of   c. in   d. with

5. Can I borrow some money _____ you? I left my wallet at home.
   a. by   b. to   c. from   d. for

6. Of course I care _____ you! I love you!
   a. with   b. to   c. of   d. about

7. Jane said she doesn't care _____ mustard, so don't put it on her sandwich.
   a. on   b. for   c. in   d. with

8. After my promotion, I was charged _____ updating the website.
   a. about   b. of   c. for   d. with

9. Both the steak and the lamb look delicious. It is hard to choose _____ them.
   a. on   b. with   c. from   d. between

10. My car slipped on the ice and I collided _____ a tree.
    a. at   b. on   c. with   d. to

11. The boss came _____ his office with an angry face and a stack of papers. I wonder why.
    a. upon   b. away   c. from   d. if

12. Do you want to comment _____ what I said?
    a. on   b. with   c. between   d. in

No. 37: communicate about

Grammar Pattern:
- **communicate about** [something]

Preposition Focus:
- We use **about** to indicate the topic of communicating.

Usage:
- People can **communicate about** a topic.

Examples:
- The HR department never **communicated about** the new employee evaluation form to us.

- Jack never **communicated** to us **about** it.

No. 38: communicate with

Grammar Pattern:
- **communicate with** [someone]

Preposition Focus:
- We use **with** to show the object of communicating.

Usage:
- A person can **communicate with** another person.

Examples:
- We **communicated with** the manager by instant messenger.

- It's difficult to **communicate with** our overseas staff because of the time difference.

No. 39: compare to

Grammar Pattern:
- **compare** [A] **to** [B]

Preposition Focus:
- We use **to** when we show the [B] that [A] is being compared with.

Usage:
- A person can **compare** one thing **to** another thing.

Examples:
- Let's **compare** this quarter's results **to** last quarter's results.
- When we **compare** this new catalog **to** last year's catalog, the new one is so much nicer.

No. 40: compare with

Grammar Pattern:
- **compare** [A] **with** [B]

Preposition Focus:
- We use **with** to show the object of comparing.

Usage:
- A person can **compare** one thing **with** another thing.

Examples:
- When we **compare** sales in June **with** sales in July, June seems much better.
- **Compared with** the trade show in Atlanta, the trade show in Las Vegas is almost three times as large.

No. 41: compete in

Grammar Pattern:
- **compete in** [something]

Preposition Focus:
- We use **in** to show the object of competing.

Usage:
- A person or company can **compete in** an event.

Examples:
- Our company is **competing in** a very competitive marketplace
- Several managers are **competing in** a golf outing this weekend.

No. 42: compete with

Grammar Pattern:
- **compete with** [someone]/[something]

Preposition Focus:
- We use **with** to show the object of competing.

Usage:
- A person or team can **compete with** other people or teams.

Examples:
- We need to successfully **compete with** ABC company in all markets.
- There are three candidates **competing with** each other for the sales manager position.

No. 43: complain about

Grammar Pattern:
- **complain about** [someone]/[something]

Preposition Focus:
- We use **about** to indicate the topic of complaining.

Usage:
- A person can **complain about** something.

Examples:
- Lou is often **complaining about** working on the weekend.
- The company has a great working atmosphere, so I really can't **complain about** working overtime sometimes.

No. 44: complain to

Grammar Pattern:
- **complain to** [someone] about [something]

Preposition Focus:
- We use **to** when we show the object of complaining.

Usage:
- A person can **complain to** another person.

Examples:
- I **complained to** the shipping company about the damaged items.
- If you **complain to** the landlord, I am sure he will fix the problem with the front door.

No. 45: compliment on

Grammar Pattern:
- **compliment** [someone] **on** [something]

Preposition Focus:
- We use **on** to show the target of complimenting.

Usage:
- A person can **compliment** another person **on** something, such as their appearance or action.

Examples:
- I **complimented** Mike **on** his successful sales trip.
- The boss **complimented** me **on** my presentation. I was so happy.

No. 46: concentrate on

Grammar Pattern:
- **concentrate on** [something]

Preposition Focus:
- We use **on** to show the target of concentrating.

Usage:
- A person can **concentrate on** something.

Examples:
- I'm going to close my office door because I need to **concentrate on** my report.
- When I am **concentrating on** something, I usually focus all of my attention on it.

No. 47: confess to

Grammar Pattern:
- **confess** [something] **to** [someone]

Preposition Focus:
- We use **to** when we show the object of confessing.

Usage:
- A person can **confess** something **to** someone.

Examples:
- Nate **confessed** his love **to** Dianna after work yesterday. I think they will get married someday!

- I had to **confess to** the boss that I am not so good at sales.

No. 48: confuse with

Grammar Pattern:
- **confuse** [A] **with** [B]

Preposition Focus:
- We use **with** to show the object of confusing.

Usage:
- A person can **confuse** one thing **with** another thing,

Examples:
- I sometimes **confuse** the sales manager **with** the marketing manager. I think they look alike.

- It's easy to **confuse** Karen **with** her twin sister Kathy. They really look alike!

Review Quiz #4

Read the sentence and choose the correct preposition (a, b, c, or d) that correctly completes the sentence.

1. Nick doesn't communicate _____ his personal life so much.
    a. of	b. in	c. with	d. about

2. We need to communicate _____ our customers more effectively.
    a. for	b. about	c. with	d. to

3. We should compare the packages _____ the sample, just to make sure they are correct.
    a. about	b. of	c. to	d. at

4. You can't compare this steak _____ the steak at AAA Restaurant. This one is much better.
    a. with	b. in	c. for	d. on

5. Yuki's sister is competing _____ a talent contest.
    a. of	b. in	c. about	d. for

6. It's difficult to compete _____ so many excellent writers.
    a. from	b. on	c. with	d. in

7. Stop complaining _____ the work. Just get it done!
    a. about	b. at	c. into	d. to

8. The store gave me a refund when I complained _____ the manager.
    a. away	b. to	c. if	d. upon

9. I must compliment you _____ this meal. Everything is delicious!
    a. with	b. between	c. in	d. on

10. Are you concentrating _____ you work, or are you daydreaming?
    a. in   b. of   c. on   d. with

11. You should confess _____ her that you don't love her anymore.
    a. to   b. on   c. for   d. by

12. I often confuse the north exit _____ the west exit of this train station.
    a. in   b. about   c. of   d. with

No. 49: congratulate for

Grammar Pattern:
- **congratulate** [someone] **for** [something]

Preposition Focus:
- We use **for** to indicate the benificiary of congratulating.

Usage:
- A person can **congratulate** another person **for** something.

Examples:
- I **congratulated** Paul **for** his promotion to supervisor.
- I **congratulated** him **for** receiving the salesman of the month award.

No. 50: congratulate on

Grammar Pattern:
- **congratulate** [someone] **on**

Preposition Focus:
- We use **on** to show the target of congratulating.

Usage:
- A person can **congratulate** another person **on** something.

Examples:
- We should **congratulate** Oscar **on** his success.
- I **congratulated** Serena **on** her promotion.

No. 51: consent to

Grammar Pattern:
- **consent to** [something]

Preposition Focus:
- We use **to** when we show the object of consenting.

Usage:
- A person can **consent to** something or doing something.

Examples:
- The boss will never **consent to** anyone taking more than two weeks vacation.
- The manager doesn't **consent to** us leaving work early on Friday.

No. 52: consist of

Grammar Pattern:
- **consist of** [something]

Preposition Focus:
- We use **of** to show the object of consisting.

Usage:
- Something **consists of** some ingredients or components.

Examples:
- The employee handbook **consists of** various rules and policies.
- My work day **consists of** checking emails and writing reports.

No. 53: contribute to

Grammar Pattern:
- **contribute to** [something]

Preposition Focus:
- We use **to** when we show the object of contributing.

Usage:
- A person can **contribute to** something.

Examples:
- Thanks for **contributing to** the project. It was a huge success.

- I was glad to see Kate **contributing** so much **to** the discussion today.

No. 54: convince of

Grammar Pattern:
- **convince** [someone] **of** [something]

Preposition Focus:
- We use **of** to show the reason for convincing.

Usage:
- A person can **convince** another person **of** something.

Examples:
- You'll never **convince** the boss **of** letting us have casual Friday in the office.

- I **convinced** him **of** cancelling the meeting tomorrow. Everyone is too busy this week.

No. 55: cope with

Grammar Pattern:
- **cope with** [something]

Preposition Focus:
- We use **with** to show the object of coping.

Usage:
- A person can **cope with** something.

Examples:
- I can't **cope with** the heat in the office. I hope they turn up the air conditioning soon.

- Jessica said she can't **cope with** working overtime every night. I agree.

No. 56: correspond with

Grammar Pattern:
- **correspond with** [someone]

Preposition Focus:
- We use **with** to show the object of corresponding.

Usage:
- A person can **correspond with** another person.

Examples:
- I've been **corresponding with** a potential customer in Germany. I hope they place an order soon.

- How can we best **correspond with** our colleagues in India?

No. 57: cover with

Grammar Pattern:
- **cover** [A] **with** [B]

Preposition Focus:
- We use **with** to show the object [B] used to cover [A].

Usage:
- A person can **cover** something **with** another thing.

Examples:
- At the end of the day I **cover** my computer **with** a dust cover.
- For Cathy's birthday, we **covered** her cake **with** chocolate covered strawberries.

No. 58: crash into

Grammar Pattern:
- **crash into** [someone]/[something]

Preposition Focus:
- We use **into** to show the object of crashing.

Usage:
- A person or a thing can **crash into** another person or thing.

Examples:
- Sam said he almost **crashed into** the manager's car when he left the parking lot yesterday.
- When I walked out of the elevator I **crashed into** my boss.

No. 59: cure of

Grammar Pattern:
- **cure** [someone] **of** [something]

Preposition Focus:
- We use **of** to show the object of curing.

Usage:
- Something can **cure** someone **of** something.

Examples:
- This medicine should **cure** you **of** your cold.

- The boss didn't give Jack a promotion this time. I think that **cured** him **of** his problem of coming to work late.

No. 60: decide against

Grammar Pattern:
- **decide against** [something]

Preposition Focus:
- We use **against** to indicate the opposition to deciding.

Usage:
- A person can **decide against** something.

Examples:
- I **decided against** asking the boss for a raise.

- I think you should **decide against** going home early today. There is too much to do.

Review Quiz #5

Read the sentence and choose the correct preposition (a, b, c, or d) that correctly completes the sentence.

1. Did you congratulate Jim _____ his achievements?
    a. for   b. in   c. to   d. on

2. I would like to congratulate you _____ getting the sale. I know you worked hard on this.
    a. about   b. to   c. for   d. of

3. Does the manager consent _____ us wearing polo shirts in the office?
    a. on   b. against   c. to   d. from

4. This emergency kit consists _____ a flashlight, radio, water, and canned food.
    a. of   b. at   c. into   d. to

5. Let me know what you can contribute _____ the meeting tomorrow.
    a. to   b. at   c. away   d. if

6. Will it be easy to convince him _____ your plans to leave early on Friday?
    a. in   b. with   c. between   d. of

7. I'm having trouble coping _____ the noise from the construction next door.
    a. with   b. of   c. in   d. about

8. Have you been corresponding _____ the Hong Kong office?
    a. for   b. with   c. by   d. to

9. This table is covered _____ a special non-stick surface.
    a. about   b. of   c. to   d. with

10. Because of the rain I crashed _____ a parked car. Thank goodness nobody was injured.
    a. into   b. in   c. for   d. on

11. That sports drink cured me _____ my sore throat. Amazing!
    a. in   b. of   c. about   d. for

12. We decided _____ going to Cancun on vacation in September because it is hurricane season.
    a. from   b. at   c. with   d. against

No. 61: decide between

Grammar Pattern:
- **decide between** [A] or [B]

Preposition Focus:
- We use **between** to indicate two things connected to deciding.

Usage:
- A person can **decide between** two things.

Examples:
- I can't **decide between** going to the Grand Canyon or Niagara Falls for my vacation.
- We have to **decide between** a Window's or Unix server.

No. 62: decide on

Grammar Pattern:
- **decide on** [something]

Preposition Focus:
- We use **on** to show the target of deciding.

Usage:
- A person can **decide on** something.

Examples:
- We need to **decide on** our next marketing plan.
- I can't **decide on** what to have for lunch.

No. 63: demand from

Grammar Pattern:
- **demand** [something] **from** [someone]

Preposition Focus:
- We use **from** to indicate the source of demanding.

Usage:
- A person can **demand** something **from** another person or a company.

Examples:
- The boss **demanded** an explanation **from** Vinny about the miscalculations in the report.
- Ethan **demanded** the truth **from** Emma about the guy she was having coffee with.

No. 64: depend on/for

Grammar Pattern:
- **depend on** [someone]/[something]

Preposition Focus:
- We use **on** to show the object of depending. We use **for** to show the benefit of **depending on** that object.

Usage:
- A person can **depend on** another person or a thing **for** something.

Examples:
- You can always **depend on** William to get his work done on time and under budget.
- I **depend on** Yalcin **for** help with computer problems.

No. 65: derive from

Grammar Pattern:
- **derive** [something] **from**

Preposition Focus:
- We use **from** to indicate the source of deriving.

Usage:
- A person can **derive** something **from** something.

Examples:
- The format of that report is not clear, so it is difficult to **derive** the information we need **from** it.
- Many English words are **derived from** Latin.

No. 66: deter from

Grammar Pattern:
- **deter** [someone] **from**

Preposition Focus:
- We use **from** to indicate the source of deterring.

Usage:
- A person or a thing can **deter** a person **from** something

Examples:
- Nothing will **deter** Adam **from** his desire to become the next CEO. He is quite determined to do it.
- Jim's father tried to **deter** him **from** taking a job overseas, but eventually, Jim went to France.

No. 67: devote to

Grammar Pattern:
- **devote to** [someone]/[something]

Preposition Focus:
- We use **to** when we show the object of devoting.

Usage:
- A person can be **devoted to** another person or a thing

Examples:
- Ben said that he **devoted** a lot of time **to** the marketing plan. I think it looks great.
- This project is important. How much time can you **devote to** it?

No. 68: differ from

Grammar Pattern:
- **differ from** [someone]/[something]

Preposition Focus:
- We use **from** to indicate the source of differing.

Usage:
- A person or a thing can **differ from** another person or thing.

Examples:
- The new marketing plan **differs** quite a lot **from** last year's plan. It has a lot of new and creative ideas.
- Even though Lucas and Jacob are twins, they **differ from** each other in many ways.

No. 69: disagree with

Grammar Pattern:
- **disagree with** [someone]/[something]

Preposition Focus:
- We use **with** to show the object of disagreeing.

Usage:
- A person can **disagree with** another person or something

Examples:
- I'm sorry to **disagree with** you, but I think investing in new trucks is not going to solve the problem completely.
- Bella often **disagrees with** her boss.

No. 70: disapprove of

Grammar Pattern:
- **disapprove of** [someone]/[something]

Preposition Focus:
- We use **of** to show the reason for disapproving.

Usage:
- A person can **disapprove of** another person or something

Examples:
- The boss **disapproves of** us taking a long lunch break.
- I **disapprove of** people smoking in a restaurant.

No. 71: discourage from

Grammar Pattern:
- **discourage** [someone] **from**

Preposition Focus:
- We use **from** to indicate the source of discouraging.

Usage:
- A person can **discourage** another person **from** doing something.

Examples:
- It would be impossible to **discourage** Chad **from** going to that concert.
- I am determined to succeed, and nothing can **discourage** me **from** working to reach my goals.

No. 72: discuss with

Grammar Pattern:
- **discuss** [A] **with** [someone]

Preposition Focus:
- We use **with** to show the person that [A] is the object of discussing.

Usage:
- A person can **discuss** something **with** another person.

Examples:
- We will be **discussing** this proposal **with** the board during the meeting on Friday.
- I **discussed** the budget **with** Amelia and she agreed that it will work.

Review Quiz #6

Read the sentence and choose the correct preposition (a, b, c, or d) that correctly completes the sentence.

1. I can't decide _____ the red and the blue tie. What do you think?
    a. into   b. at   c. between   d. to

2. We decided _____ pizza for lunch. Do you want to join us?
    a. away   b. on   c. if   d. upon

3. Our boss demands long hours _____ all of us.
    a. with   b. between   c. from   d. in

4. I can always depend _____ Nolfa _____ good advice when I am in trouble.
    a. in/of   b. of/for   c. on/for   d. with/of

5. Where is this material derived _____?
    a. to   b. from   c. for   d. by

6. He tried to deter me _____ going out in the snow.
    a. with   b. from   c. of   d. about

7. We've devoted a lot of time _____ this project. I hope it is successful.
    a. to   b. in   c. for   d. on

8. This design differs a lot _____ the old design. I hope the boss approves it.
    a. about   b. from   c. for   d. of

9. Do you often disagree _____ him?
    a. on   b. against   c. with   d. from

10. He disapproves _____ us working with music on in the office.
    a. of   b. at   c. into   d. to

11. No matter what you say, you can not discourage me _____ trying to succeed.
    a. upon   b. from   c. away   d. if

12. I need to discuss a few things _____ you after the meeting.
    a. in   b. with   c. between   d. about

No. 73: distinguish from

Grammar Pattern:
- **distinguish** [A] **from** [B]

Preposition Focus:
- We use **from** to indicate the main [A] that [B] is distinguished.

Usage:
- A person can **distinguish** one person or thing **from** another person or thing.

Examples:
- It's not difficult to **distinguish** the new $100 bills **from** the old ones.
- Sofia and her sister are identical twins. It is impossible to **distinguish** one **from** the other.

No. 74: distract from

Grammar Pattern:
- **distract** [someone] **from** [something]

Preposition Focus:
- We use **from** to indicate the source of distraction.

Usage:
- A person or a thing can **distract** another person **from** something.

Examples:
- The loud music is **distracting** me **from** completing this report. I hope the party ends soon.
- The barking dogs **distracted** Daniel **from** concentrating on his homework.

No. 75: dream about

Grammar Pattern:
- **dream about** [someone]/[something]

Preposition Focus:
- We use **about** to indicate the topic of dreaming while sleeping.

Usage:
- A person can **dream about** another person or something.

Examples:
- Craig has **dreamed about** his promotion since last year. I'm glad he got it.
- I **dreamed about** my grandmother last night.

No. 76: dream of

Grammar Pattern:
- **dream of** [someone]/[something]

Preposition Focus:
- We use **of** to show the object of dreaming.

Usage:
- A person can **dream of** something. Dream of has the meaning of "invent" or "create in the mind" or "hope for."

Examples:
- I **dream of** the day I can leave here and start my own company.
- Do you like my new invention? I **dreamed of** it while I was at the beach.

No. 77: dress in (1)

Grammar Pattern:
- **dress in** [something]

Preposition Focus:
- We use **in** to show the object of dressing.

Usage:
- A person can **dress in** something.

Examples:
- Everyone is going to **dress in** suits for the meeting next week.
- We are allowed to **dress in** jeans on Fridays.

No. 78: dress in (2)

Grammar Pattern:
- **dress** [someone] **in** [something]

Preposition Focus:
- We use **in** to show the object of dressing.

Usage:
- A person can **dress** another person (or a pet) **in** something.

Examples:
- Danny **dressed** his son **in** a blue suit for the wedding. He looked so cute.
- Keiko **dressed** her dog **in** a Halloween costume this year.

No. 79: drink to

Grammar Pattern:
- **drink to** [someone]/[something]

Preposition Focus:
- We use **to** when we show the object of drinking. "Drink to" is usually used when drinking alcohol and saying "cheers."

Usage:
- A person can **drink to** another person or thing.

Examples:
- Let's raise our glasses and **drink to** another 25 successful years of ABC Company.
- The boss is retiring? I'll **drink to** that!

No. 80: elaborate on

Grammar Pattern:
- **elaborate on** [something]

Preposition Focus:
- We use **on** to show the target of elaborating.

Usage:
- A person can **elaborate on** something.

Examples:
- Thanks for the information. Can you **elaborate on** your plan to expand the company's operations in Asia?
- During the meeting, Ryan **elaborated on** the company's plan to open a new office in San Diego.

No. 81: emerge from

Grammar Pattern:
- **emerge from** [something]

Preposition Focus:
- We use **from** to indicate the source of emerging.

Usage:
- A person can **emerge from** something.

Examples:
- BCD Company **emerged from** bankruptcy healthy and ready for its next phase of doing business.
- A man on a horse **emerged from** the foggy forest.

No. 82: escape from

Grammar Pattern:
- **escape from** [someone]/[something]

Preposition Focus:
- We use **from** to indicate the source of escaping.

Usage:
- A person or an animal can **escape from** another person or a place.

Examples:
- Fred tried to **escape from** the dinner meeting, but the boss told him he had to attend.
- My dog often tries to **escape from** her leash.

No. 83: exchange for

Grammar Pattern:
- **exchange** [A] **for** [B]

Preposition Focus:
- We use **for** to indicate the [B] that is the purpose of exchanging [A].

Usage:
- A person can **exchange** one thing **for** another thing.

Examples:
- We are going to **exchange** this old copy machine **for** a new one next week.
- I have to **exchange** this sweater **for** one that is a larger size.

No. 84: exclude from

Grammar Pattern:
- **exclude** [A] **from** [something]

Preposition Focus:
- We use **from** to indicate the main [A] that [B] is excluded.

Usage:
- A person can **exclude** someone or something **from** something.

Examples:
- The boss **excluded** George **from** the meeting because he is not involved with this project.
- We have to **exclude** a few items **from** the budget, otherwise it won't get approved.

Review Quiz #7

Read the sentence and choose the correct preposition (a, b, c, or d) that correctly completes the sentence.

1. Can you distinguish the real bag _____ the fake one?
    a. from b. of c. in d. with

2. Did the noise outside distract you _____ working?
    a. for b. from c. by d. to

3. Dan said he dreams _____ retiring on a tropical island somewhere.
    a. to b. at c. about d. with

4. I dreamed _____ this idea when I was skiing in Colorado.
    a. of b. in c. for d. on

5. Do you dress _____ a suit and tie every day?
    a. of b. in c. about d. for

6. I was dressed _____ jeans all week during my vacation.
    a. from b. in c. against d. on

7. Let's drink _____ having a successful business trip this week.
    a. into b. to c. in d. at

8. I think I understand, but can you elaborate _____ your plan a little more?
    a. away b. on c. if d. upon

9. Bob emerged _____ the meeting with an upset look on his face.
    a. with b. between c. from d. in

78

10. Help me! The cat escaped _____ the house.
    a. from   b. of   c. in   d. with

11. Can you exchange this tie _____ another one? I have my receipt right here.
    a. to   b. for   c. of   d. by

12. We need to exclude 2 people _____ the meeting.
    a. with   b. about   c. from   d. of

No. 85: excuse for

Grammar Pattern:
- **excuse** [someone] **for** [something]

Preposition Focus:
- We use **for** to indicate the purpose of excusing.

Usage:
- A person can **excuse** themselves **for** something.

Examples:
- Please **excuse** me **for** bothering you, but this meeting room has been reserved. Please use meeting room B.
- Can you **excuse** me **for** a moment? I have to make a quick phone call.

No. 86: excuse from

Grammar Pattern:
- **excuse** [someone] **from** [something]

Preposition Focus:
- We use **from** to indicate the source of excusing.

Usage:
- A person can **excuse** another person **from** something, such as an event like a party or a meeting.

Examples:
- The boss **excused** me **from** the meeting because he wants me to work on another project.
- We should **excuse** Hannah **from** attending the workshop. She's already got those skills.

No. 87: expel from

Grammar Pattern:
- **expel** [someone] **from** [something]

Preposition Focus:
- We use **from** to indicate the source of expelling.

Usage:
- A person can **expel** someone **from** somewhere.

Examples:
- The principal **expelled** Bob **from** school for hitting a teacher.
- I **expelled** him **from** the meeting after he threw the remote control at me.

No. 88: experiment on

Grammar Pattern:
- **experiment on** [someone]/[something]

Preposition Focus:
- We use **on** to show the target of experimenting.

Usage:
- A person can **experiment on** another living thing.

Examples:
- That company **experiments on** mice to test new cosmetics.
- I think that crazy doctor wanted to **experiment on** me!

No. 89: experiment with

Grammar Pattern:
- **experiment with** [something]

Preposition Focus:
- We use **with** to show the object of experimenting.

Usage:
- A person can **experiment with** some materials or ingredients.

Examples:
- I'm going to **experiment with** this script to see if it works with the server correctly.
- Daniel said he **experimented with** a few different templates before he found this one.

No. 90: explain to

Grammar Pattern:
- **explain** [topic] **to** [someone]

Preposition Focus:
- We use **to** when we show the person receiving the explanation.

Usage:
- A person can **explain** something **to** another person.

Examples:
- I tried to **explain** the policy **to** Ida, but she didn't understand it completely.
- Andy is a bright guy. You only need to **explain** something **to** him once.

No. 91: face with

Grammar Pattern:
- **face with** [something]

Preposition Focus:
- We use **with** to show the object of facing.

Usage:
- A person or group can be **faced with** a negative or bad situation.

Examples:
- We are **faced with** a large budget deficit, so we have to cut expenses.
- Because the company is **faced with** declining sales, they are going to lay off 10% of their workforce.

No. 92: feel about

Grammar Pattern:
- **feel** [adjective] **about** [something]

Preposition Focus:
- We use **about** to indicate the topic of feeling.

Usage:
- A person can **feel** a certain way **about** a situation.

Examples:
- We all **felt** happy **about** Yumi's promotion to VP of sales.
- How would you **feel about** transferring to our sister company in Singapore?

No. 93: feel for

Grammar Pattern:
- **feel** [adjective] **for** [something]

Preposition Focus:
- We use **for** to indicate the benificiary of feeling.

Usage:
- A person can **feel** a certain way **for** another person

Examples:
- We all **felt** happy **for** Satomi. She got a promotion to office manager.
- I **feel** bad **for** Joe. His girlfriend left him for another guy.

No. 94: fight against

Grammar Pattern:
- **fight against** [someone]/[something]

Preposition Focus:
- We use **against** to indicate the opposition to fighting.

Usage:
- A person can **fight against** another person or a situation.

Examples:
- In Europe, we are **fighting against** a number of strong competitors.
- If you try to **fight against** a customer, you will surely loose.

No. 95: fight for

Grammar Pattern:
- **fight for** [something]

Preposition Focus:
- We use **for** to indicate the purpose of fighting.

Usage:
- A person can **fight for** something they want or believe in.

Examples:
- If you are willing to **fight for** your proposal, I think eventually the boss will approve it.
- Max **fought for** the promotion and eventually became the manager.

No. 96: fight with

Grammar Pattern:
- **fight with** [someone]/[something]

Preposition Focus:
- We use **with** to show the object of fighting.

Usage:
- A person can **fight with** another person.

Examples:
- You will never win a **fight with** a customer.
- I wouldn't **fight with** the boss. He's very stubborn.

Review Quiz #8

Read the sentence and choose the correct preposition (a, b, c, or d) that correctly completes the sentence.

1. Excuse me _____ a few minutes. I need to make a phone call.
    a. for   b. in   c. by   d. on

2. I was excused _____ the meeting because I need to finish this report.
    a. about   b. from   c. for   d. of

3. Why was Jen's daughter expelled _____ school?
    a. on   b. against   c. to   d. from

4. We are experimenting _____ a few different ways to solve this issue.
    a. on   b. at   c. into   d. to

5. Why don't you experiment _____ a few different shades of blue and see which one looks the best.
    a. upon   b. with   c. away   d. if

6. I explained _____ him several times but he is being stubborn about his decision.
    a. in   b. with   c. between   d. to

7. We are faced _____ strong competition in Latin America.
    a. at   b. of   c. with   d. in

8. How do you feel _____ working at the LA office for a few weeks?
    a. for   b. about   c. by   d. to

9. I feel so happy _____ Kevin. He's going to be the new director.
        a. about   b. of   c. for   d. with

10. I was fighting _____ a strong wind on the way into the office. It was hard to walk!
        a. against   b. about   c. for   d. of

11. If you want to get approval for this, you are going to need to fight _____ it.
        a. on   b. for   c. against   d. from

12. Len said he has been fighting _____ his wife for a long time.
        a. into   b. to   c. at   d. with

No. 97: forget about

Grammar Pattern:
- **forget about** [someone]/[something]

Preposition Focus:
- We use **about** to indicate the topic of forgetting.

Usage:
- A person can **forget about** another person or situation.

Examples:
- I totally **forgot about** the meeting this morning.
- Anna said she finally **forgot about** her ex-boyfriend completely.

No. 98: forgive for

Grammar Pattern:
- **forgive** [someone] **for** [something]

Preposition Focus:
- We use **for** to indicate the purpose of forgiving

Usage:
- A person can **forgive** another person **for** something.

Examples:
- Please **forgive** me **for** interrupting your meeting. There is an urgent phone call for Jack.
- Lucy said she would never **forgive** him **for** cheating on her.

No. 99: get married to

Grammar Pattern:
- **get married to** [someone]

Preposition Focus:
- We use **to** when we show the person getting married.

Usage:
- A person can **get married to** another person.

Examples:
- I heard that Kevin is **getting married to** a lawyer.

- Conner **got married to** a woman from Brazil.

No. 100: graduate from

Grammar Pattern:
- **graduate from** [a school]

Preposition Focus:
- We use **from** to indicate the school of graduating.

Usage:
- A person can **graduate from** a school.

Examples:
- The sales manager **graduated from** Colombia University.

- When I **graduate from** this school, I'm going to spend a year traveling abroad.

No. 101: grumble about

Grammar Pattern:
- **grumble about** [something]

Preposition Focus:
- We use **about** to indicate the topic of grumbling.

Usage:
- A person can **grumble about** something.

Examples:
- Lenny is always **grumbling about** his workload.

- Everyone in the office has been **grumbling about** working overtime.

No. 102: guess at

Grammar Pattern:
- **guess at** [something]

Preposition Focus:
- We use **at** to indicate the target point of guessing.

Usage:
- A person can **guess at** something.

Examples:
- It's sometimes difficult to **guess at** what the boss wants.

- Have you ever tried to **guess at** what your spouse is thinking?

No. 103: happen to

Grammar Pattern:
- **happen to** [someone]/[something]

Preposition Focus:
- We use **to** when we show the object of happening.

Usage:
- Something can **happen to** a person or thing.

Examples:
- Something **happened to** the server this morning.
- What **happened to** your hair? It's orange!

No. 104: hear about

Grammar Pattern:
- **hear about** [someone]/[something]

Preposition Focus:
- We use **about** to indicate the topic of hearing.

Usage:
- A person can **hear about** another person or something.

Examples:
- Everyone **heard about** Mary's promotion. How wonderful!
- Did you **hear about** the meeting? It was a huge success.

No. 105: hear from

Grammar Pattern:
- **hear from** [someone]

Preposition Focus:
- We use **from** to indicate the source of hearing.

Usage:
- A person can **hear from** another person.

Examples:
- We have finally **heard from** all of the branch managers, so let's decide on the next steps.
- I haven't **heard from** my aunt in a while. I think I'll give her a call.

No. 106: hear of

Grammar Pattern:
- **hear of** [someone]/[something]

Preposition Focus:
- We use **of** to show the object of hearing.

Usage:
- A person can **hear of** another person or something.

Examples:
- Have you ever **heard of** cloud computing?
- I never **heard of** Lou Reed until my sister gave me his CD.

No. 107: help with

Grammar Pattern:
- **help** [someone] **with** [something]

Preposition Focus:
- We use **with** to show the object of helping.

Usage:
- A person can **help** another person **with** something.

Examples:
- Can you **help** me **with** the marketing plan?
- I **helped** Tyler **with** his homework. I think he understands it now.

No. 108: hide from

Grammar Pattern:
- **hide from** [someone] or [hide something] from [someone]

Preposition Focus:
- We use **from** to indicate the source of hiding.

Usage:
- A person can **hide from** another person or **hide** something **from** another person.

Examples:
- Nick wants to **hide from** Kate. I think she rejected is offer for a date.
- I think Chris should **hide** her tattoo **from** the CEO when he visits next week.

Review Quiz #9

Read the sentence and choose the correct preposition (a, b, c, or d) that correctly completes the sentence.

1. Please don't forget _____ our appointment tomorrow!
    a. away	b. about	c. if	d. upon

2. I will never forgive her _____ cheating on me.
    a. between	b. with	c. in	d. for

3. He's going to finally get married _____ her, after 10 years of dating.
    a. at	b. of	c. for	d. to

4. This guy has a good resume, but he never graduated _____ university.
    a. for	b. from	c. by	d. to

5. What is Jim grumbling _____ now?
    a. about	b. with	c. of	d. on

6. Don't try to guess _____ the problem. Get the IT department to work on your computer.
    a. for	b. on	c. at	d. in

7. I wonder what happened _____ Nick. He hasn't called us all week.
    a. at	b. about	c. for	d. to

8. I heard _____ the accident. At lease nobody was hurt.
    a. against	b. from	c. about	d. on

9. We haven't heard _____ you, Conner. What is your opinion?
    a. to	b. from	c. at	d. into

10. Did you ever hear _____ a "cronut?" It's a combination of a donut and a croissant.
    a. to   b. of   c. if   d. upon

11. Do you think you can help me _____ moving this cabinet?
    a. with   b. about   c. between   d. in

12. I was late this morning. I'd better hide _____ the manager.
    a. from   b. with   c. of   d. in

No. 109: hinder from

Grammar Pattern:
- **hinder** [someone] **from**

Preposition Focus:
- We use **from** to indicate the source of hindering.

Usage:
- Something can **hinder** a person **from** doing something.

Examples:
- This broken keyboard is **hindering** me **from** getting my work done.
- Something is **hindering** Kyle **from** finishing his work. I wonder what it is.

No. 110: hope for

Grammar Pattern:
- **hope for** [something]

Preposition Focus:
- We use **for** to indicate the purpose of hoping.

Usage:
- A person can **hope for** something.

Examples:
- Della said she is **hoping for** a promotion when she meets with the boss tomorrow.
- John said he is **hoping for** a change in the weather. There is a big golf game tomorrow.

No. 111: impress on

Grammar Pattern:
- **impress on** [someone]

Preposition Focus:
- We use **on** to show the target of impressing.

Usage:
- A person can **impress** something **on** another person.

Examples:
- I tried to **impress on** the boss the importance of upgrading the server.
- It was impossible to **impress on** her the reasons for the change in policy.

No. 112: insist on

Grammar Pattern:
- **insist on** [something]

Preposition Focus:
- We use **on** to show the target of insisting.

Usage:
- A person can **insist on** something.

Examples:
- I **insisted on** meeting with the manager in order to resolve the problem.
- Brandon **insisted on** everyone in the office joining him for dinner.

No. 113: insure against

Grammar Pattern:
- **insure against** [something]

Preposition Focus:
- We use **against** to indicate the opposition to insuring.

Usage:
- Something or a person can **insure against** something bad.

Examples:
- This cloud backup system will **insure against** data loss.
- The extra cushioning in this box will **insure against** breakage during transit.

No. 114: interfere in

Grammar Pattern:
- **interfere in** [something]

Preposition Focus:
- We use **in** to show the object of interfering.

Usage:
- A person can **interfere in** another person's situation.

Examples:
- You should never **interfere in** a coworker's personal situation.
- Again Peter **interfered in** my work! He is such a micro-manager.

No. 115: interfere with

Grammar Pattern:
- **interfere with** [someone]/[something]

Preposition Focus:
- We use **with** to show the object of interfering.

Usage:
- Something or a person can **interfere with** a person or something.

Examples:
- The noise from the server is **interfering with** my ability to concentrate on my work.
- The steel and brick in this old building **interferes with** the cell phone signal. It's really hard to make a call here.

No. 116: introduce to

Grammar Pattern:
- **introduce** [someone] **to** [someone else]

Preposition Focus:
- We use **to** when we show the person being introduced.

Usage:
- A person can **introduce** another person **to** a third person.

Examples:
- I **introduced** the chairman **to** all of the managers.
- Naomi said that she would **introduce** her friend **to** me next week.

No. 117: invest in

Grammar Pattern:
- **invest in** [someone]/[something]

Preposition Focus:
- We use **in** to show the object of investing.

Usage:
- A person can **invest in** something.

Examples:
- The company is finally going to **invest in** new laptop computers for the whole staff.
- I'm thinking of **investing in** stocks and bonds.

No. 118: invite for

Grammar Pattern:
- **invite** [someone] **for**

Preposition Focus:
- We use **for** to indicate the purpose of inviting.

Usage:
- A person can **invite** another person **for** an event.

Examples:
- Let's **invite** the manager **for** drinks. Tomorrow is his birthday.
- My customer **invited** me **for** lunch today.

No. 119: invite to

Grammar Pattern:
- **invite** [someone] **to**

Preposition Focus:
- We use **to** when we show the event which someone is invited for.

Usage:
- A person can **invite** another person **to** an event.

Examples:
- The boss **invited** our best customers **to** the golf outing.
- We were **invited to** a Halloween party. I am looking forward to going.

No. 120: involve in

Grammar Pattern:
- **involve** [someone] **in**

Preposition Focus:
- We use **in** to show the object of involving.

Usage:
- A person can **involve** another person **in** a situation or event, or be involved in a situation or event.

Examples:
- The boss **involved** me **in** the budget planning process.
- I wasn't **involved in** the planning meeting, so I am not sure what they discussed.

Review Quiz #10

Read the sentence and choose the correct preposition (a, b, c, or d) that correctly completes the sentence.

1. This pain in my ankle is hindering me _____ walking quickly.
    a. from b. for c. by d. to

2. Let's hope _____ a change in the weather by this afternoon.
    a. of b. for c. with d. about

3. He impressed the importance of this report _____ me quite clearly.
    a. of b. in c. on d. for

4. Brad insisted _____ paying for lunch. What a nice guy.
    a. of b. about c. for d. on

5. This wrapping will insure _____ damage to the statue.
    a. on b. from c. for d. against

6. Please don't interfere _____ our personal problems.
    a. into b. to c. at d. in

7. Something is interfering _____ the cell phone signal in this building. I can't make a call.
    a. with b. away c. if d. upon

8. Can you introduce me _____ your IT manager?
    a. between b. to c. in d. with

9. We are investing a lot of effort _____ this new project.
    a. with b. of c. in d. on

10. I'd like to invite you and your wife _____ dinner on Saturday. Are you available?
    a. of   b. for   c. by   d. on

11. I was just invited _____ the sales conference next week in Vegas.
    a. about   b. with   c. of   d. to

12. Let me know if you need help. I've been involved _____ that kind of deployment before.
    a. for   b. on   c. of   d. in

Special Bonus Lesson: Prepositions With Made

Made is an interesting English verb because it collocates with a number of different prepositions. Let's have a look at these combinations of made and prepositions with some examples:

We use **made in** to show the place of origin of an object.
- That TV was **made in** the USA.
- These days, Volkswagens that are sold **in** the USA are **made in** Mexico.
- I bought some pretzels that were **made in** Brooklyn.

We use **made of** to show the material that an object is manufactured or produced from:
- This desk is **made of** wood.
- Many items these days are **made of** plastic.
- That looks like glass, but it is actually **made of** vinyl.

We use **made with** to show the ingredients in something, generally food:
- This is all natural ice cream. It's **made with** milk, cream, sugar and vanilla.
- Don't eat those cookies. They are **made with** a lot of artificial chemicals.
- This BBQ sauce is **made with** tomatoes, spices, and several secret ingredients.

We also use **made from** to show the ingredients in something, generally food:
- This is all natural ice cream. It's **made from** milk, cream, sugar and vanilla.
- Don't eat those cookies. They are **made from** a lot of artificial chemicals.
- This BBQ sauce is **made from** tomatoes, spices, and several secret ingredients.

We use **made by** to show the process or people used to manufacture or produce something:
- These apple pies are **made by** hand.
- Candy bars are **made by** machines in a factory.
- That jewelry was **made by** Native Americans.

No. 121: joke about

Grammar Pattern:
- **joke about** [someone]/[something]

Preposition Focus:
- We use **about** to indicate the topic of joking.

Usage:
- A person can **joke about** another person or thing.

Examples:
- Brad got in trouble when he **joked about** the boss in front of the office manager.
- Don't **joke about** Della's ex-boyfriend. She is very sensitive about that topic.

No. 122: joke with

Grammar Pattern:
- **joke with** [someone]

Preposition Focus:
- We use **with** to show the person joking together with.

Usage:
- A person can **joke with** another person.

Examples:
- The manager is a very serious guy, not the type of person you can **joke with**.
- I was **joking with** my sister during dinner last night. We had a great time.

No. 123: keep for

Grammar Pattern:
- **keep** [something] **for** [someone]

Preposition Focus:
- We use **for** to indicate the purpose of keeping.

Usage:
- A person can **keep** something **for** another person or time.

Examples:
- I'm **keeping** this last catalog **for** the marketing manager.
- Don't use that bottle of champagne. Let's **keep** it **for** a special occasion.

No. 124: keep away from

Grammar Pattern:
- **keep away from** [someone]/[something]

Preposition Focus:
- We use **from** to indicate the source of keeping away.

Usage:
- A person can **keep away from** another person or thing.

Examples:
- If I were you, I would keep **away from** the boss today. He's in a bad mood.
- I like to eat healthy food, so I keep **away from** fast food restaurants.

No. 125: know about

Grammar Pattern:
- **know about** [someone]/[something]

Preposition Focus:
- We use **about** to indicate the topic of knowing.

Usage:
- A person can **know about** another person or something.

Examples:
- Do you **know about** the new vacation policy?
- I didn't **know about** Bob's retirement. When did he announce that?

No. 126: laugh about

Grammar Pattern:
- **laugh about** [someone]/[something]

Preposition Focus:
- We use **about** to indicate the topic of laughing.

Usage:
- A person can **laugh about** another person or something.

Examples:
- We were all **laughing about** Dan's story about his missing keys.
- I can **laugh about** the accident now, but it wasn't funny when it happened.

No. 127: laugh at

Grammar Pattern:
- **laugh at** [someone]/[something]

Preposition Focus:
- We use **at** to indicate the target point of laughing.

Usage:
- A person can **laugh at** another person.

Examples:
- Don't **laugh at** me. I am working as quickly as possible.
- Everyone **laughed at** John when he said that he was too shy to ask Mary for a date.

No. 128: learn about

Grammar Pattern:
- **learn about** [someone]/[something]

Preposition Focus:
- We use **about** to indicate the topic of learning.

Usage:
- A person can **learn about** another person or something.

Examples:
- I **learned about** Eri's termination from the receptionist.
- Joe said that he **learned** a lot **about** fixing computers from his father.

No. 129: leave for

Grammar Pattern:
- **leave for** [place]

Preposition Focus:
- We use **for** to indicate the destination which is the purpose of leaving.

Usage:
- A person or vehicle can **leave for** a place.

Examples:
- This plane **leaves for** Paris at 9:00am.
- We are **leaving for** the trade show tomorrow.

No. 130: leave from

Grammar Pattern:
- **leave from** [place]

Preposition Focus:
- We use **from** to indicate the place of departure.

Usage:
- A person or vehicle can **leave from** a place.

Examples:
- We **left from** JFK airport at 10:00.
- When we **leave from** here we will have lots of wonderful memories!

No. 131: lend to

Grammar Pattern:
- **lend** [something] **to**

Preposition Focus:
- We use **to** when we show the person the object is lent.

Usage:
- A person can **lend** something **to** another person.

Examples:
- I **lent** my fountain pen **to** the accounting manager at the meeting.
- Can you **lend** your golf clubs **to** Jake? He wants to join the golf outing tomorrow.

No. 132: listen for

Grammar Pattern:
- **listen for** [someone]/[something]

Preposition Focus:
- We use **for** to indicate the purpose of listening.

Usage:
- A person can **listen for** another person or something.

Examples:
- When you call, **listen for** the beep and then press the pound key.
- I am trying to **listen for** information about the hurricane, but so far the news hasn't said anything.

Review Quiz #11

Read the sentence and choose the correct preposition (a, b, c, or d) that correctly completes the sentence.

1. The downturn in sales is nothing to joke _____. It's a big problem.
    a. about   b. away   c. for   d. of

2. They are often joking _____ their coworkers.
    a. against   b. with   c. from   d. on

3. I am keeping this tie _____ a special occasion.
    a. upon   b. away   c. for   d. if

4. I have to keep away _____ that snack vending machine in the afternoons.
    a. from   b. at   c. into   d. to

5. I've known _____ the trouble for a few hours, that's why I've been trying to contact you.
    a. with   b. in   c. between d. about

6. What are you laughing _____? You guys are so loud!
    a. in   b. with   c. of   d. about

7. Don't laugh _____ me, ok? I'm having a tough time with my hair today.
    a. at   b. for   c. by   d. to

8. I learned a lot _____ marketing from Gary.
    a. of   b. for   c. with   d. about

9. When are you leaving _____ Taipei?
    a. of   b. for   c. in   d. with

10. We left _____ the hotel at 5:00am because we had an early flight
    a. from   b. to   c. of   d. with

11. Who did you lend the projector _____? I need it for the meeting tomorrow.
    a. on   b. to   c. in   d. for

12. The mechanic took my car for a ride so he could listen _____ the noise.
    a. for   b. of   c. about   d. with

No. 133: listen to

Grammar Pattern:
- **listen to** [something]

Preposition Focus:
- We use **to** when we show the object **of** listening.

Usage:
- A person can **listen to** another person or something.

Examples:
- We need to **listen to** the results of the sales promotion carefully.
- **Listen to** your mother. Her advice is always the best.

No. 134: long for

Grammar Pattern:
- **long for** [someone]/[something]

Preposition Focus:
- We use **for** to indicate the purpose of longing.

Usage:
- A person can **long for** another person or something.

Examples:
- I've been working a lot of overtime. I am **longing for** a vacation.
- I have been **longing for** delicious pizza ever since I saw that documentary about pizza on TV.

No. 135: look at

Grammar Pattern:
- **look at** [someone]/[something]

Preposition Focus:
- We use **at** to indicate the target point of looking.

Usage:
- A person can **look at** another person or something.

Examples:
- I am going to **look at** the report this afternoon.
- I need to **look at** that photo once more. I think I recognize somebody in the photo.

No. 136: look for

Grammar Pattern:
look for [someone]/[something]

Preposition Focus:
- We use **for** to indicate the purpose of looking.

Usage:
- A person can **look for** another person or something.

Examples:
- The boss is **looking for** Jack, have you seen him?
- I **looked** everywhere **for** my keys, but I can't find them.

No. 137: matter to

Grammar Pattern:
- **matter to** [someone]

Preposition Focus:
- We use **to** when we show the object of mattering.

Usage:
- Something **matters to** a person.

Examples:
- It doesn't **matter to** me where we have the dinner meeting.
- Does it **matter to** you if we finish this work tomorrow? I need to go home early today.

No. 138: meet with

Grammar Pattern:
- **meet with** [someone]/[something]

Preposition Focus:
- We use **with** to show the object of meeting.

Usage:
- A person can **meet with** another person or a situation.

Examples:
- I'm **meeting with** Harry on Thursday.
- Since I decided to expand the business, I need to **meet with** my accountant and my lawyer.

No. 139: mistake for

Grammar Pattern:
- **mistake** [A] **for** [B]

Preposition Focus:
- We use **for** to indicate the [B] that [A] is mistaken for.

Usage:
- A person can **mistake** someone or something **for** another person or thing.

Examples:
- Bob said he almost **mistook** the email from the CEO **for** a similar email from the HR director.
- Be careful not to **mistake** your suitcase **for** another person's suitcase at the airport.

No. 140: object to

Grammar Pattern:
- **object to** [someone]/[something]

Preposition Focus:
- We use **to** when we show the object of objection.

Usage:
- A person can **object to** another person or something.

Examples:
- I don't **object to** working overtime, but only if it is a few days per month.
- Gloria said she **objects to** our using cell phones at the dinner table.

No. 141: operate with

Grammar Pattern:
- **operate with** [something]

Preposition Focus:
- We use **with** to show the object of operating.

Usage:
- A person or a thing can **operate with** something.

Examples:
- This laptop computer **operates with** lithium batteries.
- That toy **operates with** a small, solar powered motor.

No. 142: participate in

Grammar Pattern:
- **participate in** [something]

Preposition Focus:
- We use **in** to show the object of participating.

Usage:
- A person can **participate in** some event.

Examples:
- I was asked to **participate in** the teacher's conference next week.
- Are you **participating in** the trade show in Dallas?

No. 143: pay for

Grammar Pattern:
- **pay for** [someone]/[something]

Preposition Focus:
- We use **for** to indicate the purpose of paying.

Usage:
- A person can **pay for** something.

Examples:
- It's your birthday, so I'll **pay for** dinner tonight.
- Who is going to **pay for** lunch today? I paid last time.

No. 144: persist in

Grammar Pattern:
- **persist in** + VerbING (gerund)

Preposition Focus:
- We use **in** to show the object of persisting.

Usage:
- A person can **persist in** doing something.

Examples:
- Glenn **persisted in** arguing with the boss, but his persistence accomplished nothing.
- If you **persist in** bothering me about a raise, you certainly won't get one.

Review Quiz #12

Read the sentence and choose the correct preposition (a, b, c, or d) that correctly completes the sentence.

1. Why don't you listen _____ me when I give you advice?
   - a. to
   - b. against
   - c. from
   - d. on

2. I'm really longing _____ some bread. This no-carb diet is really difficult!
   - a. at
   - b. for
   - c. into
   - d. to

3. I've been looking _____ the clock all day. This day is going so slowly!
   - a. upon
   - b. away
   - c. if
   - d. at

4. What are you looking _____? Maybe I can help you.
   - a. for
   - b. between
   - c. in
   - d. with

5. It doesn't matter _____ me where we go, as long as there is a beach.
   - a. with
   - b. to
   - c. of
   - d. in

6. I'm going to meet _____ Eri tomorrow. Do you have any messages for her?
   - a. by
   - b. to
   - c. with
   - d. for

7. He mistook the statement _____ an invoice, and accidentally paid it!
   - a. for
   - b. of
   - c. with
   - d. about

8. I object _____ working every weekend.
   - a. in
   - b. to
   - c. for
   - d. on

9. My cordless mouse operates _____ two AA batteries. Do you have any of those?
   - a. of
   - b. about
   - c. with
   - d. for

10. I've participated _____ several of those workshops. I like them!
    a. in   b. against   c. from   d. on

11. I need to pay _____ this round of drinks before leaving the bar.
    a. for   b. with   c. at   d. into

12. She persisted _____ telling me her whole life story.
    a. in   b. upon   c. away   d. to

No. 145: plan on

Grammar Pattern:
- **plan on** [something]

Preposition Focus:
- We use **on** to show the target of planning.

Usage:
- A person can **plan on** something.

Examples:
- I'm **planning on** walking to the office in order to get some exercise.
- When are you **planning on** telling Bob that he got the promotion?

No. 146: praise for

Grammar Pattern:
- **praise** [someone] **for** [something]

Preposition Focus:
- We use **for** to indicate the purpose of praising.

Usage:
- A person can **praise** another person **for** something.

Examples:
- The CEO **praised** the management team **for** their successful sales results.
- The manager should **praise** his staff **for** completing the project in time and under budget.

No. 147: pray for

Grammar Pattern:
- **pray for** [someone/something]

Preposition Focus:
- We use **for** to indicate the purpose of praying.

Usage:
- A person can **pray for** something.

Examples:
- Hank said that in his church they often **pray for** world peace.
- The office golf game is tomorrow. **Pray for** rain. I don't want **to** go!

No. 148: pray to

Grammar Pattern:
- **pray to** [god/deity]

Preposition Focus:
- We use **to** when we show the object of praying.

Usage:
- A person can **pray to** a deity or God.

Examples:
- Many people **pray to** God in very different ways.
- In ancient times, some cultures **prayed to** the sun and the moon.

No. 149: prefer to

Grammar Pattern:
- **prefer** [A] **to** [B]

Preposition Focus:
- We use **to** when we show the [B] that [A] is preferred.

Usage:
- A person can prefer one thing or person **to** another thing or person.

Examples:
- I **prefer** Mac OS computers **to** Windows computers.
- I **prefer** eating out **to** cooking dinner at home tonight. I'm too tired to cook.

No. 150: prepare for

Grammar Pattern:
- **prepare for** [something]

Preposition Focus:
- We use **for** to indicate the purpose of preparing.

Usage:
- A person can **prepare for** something.

Examples:
- Everyone is busy **preparing for** tomorrow's sales meeting.
- Are you **prepared for** your business trip to Bangkok?

No. 151: present with

Grammar Pattern:
- present [someone] **with** [something]

Preposition Focus:
- We use **with** to show the object being presented.

Usage:
- A person can **present** another person **with** something.

Examples:
- The chairman **presented** the CEO **with** an award for 40 years of service to the company.
- He **presented** me **with** a gold watch when I retired.

No. 152: prevent from

Grammar Pattern:
- **prevent** [someone] from

Preposition Focus:
- We use **from** to indicate the source of preventing.

Usage:
- A person can **prevent** another person **from** doing something.

Examples:
- Our plan is very good. I think nothing can **prevent** us **from** being successful.
- The bad weather **prevented** our flight **from** departing on time.

No. 153: prohibit from

Grammar Pattern:
- **prohibit** [someone] **from** [something]

Preposition Focus:
- We use **from** to indicate the source of prohibiting.

Usage:
- A person or rule can **prevent** another person **from** doing something.

Examples:
- Company policy **prohibits** employees **from** wearing jeans to work.
- We were **prohibited from** entering that room, but I am not sure why.

No. 154: protect from

Grammar Pattern:
- **protect** [A] **from** [B]

Preposition Focus:
- We use **from** to indicate the source of protecting.

Usage:
- Something or a person can **protect** something or someone **from** something bad.

Examples:
- This battery backup will **protect** the server **from** data loss in the event of a power failure.
- These goggles will **protect** your eyes **from** injury when you work in the factory.

No. 155: provide for

Grammar Pattern:
- **provide for** [someone] or **provide** [something] **for** [someone]

Preposition Focus:
- We use **for** to indicate the purpose of providing.

Usage:
- A person can **provide for** another person.

Examples:
- Maria is able to **provide for** her children well because she has a high salary.
- We need to **provide** space **for** fifty people visiting from our sister company in Miami.

No. 156: provide with

Grammar Pattern:
- **provide** [someone] **with** [something]

Preposition Focus:
- We use **with** to show the object being provided.

Usage:
- An organization or a person can **provide** something or someone **with** something.

Examples:
- The company **provides** all employees **with** a laptop computer and a smartphone.
- The airline **provides** business class travelers **with** noise cancelling headphones.

Review Quiz #13

Read the sentence and choose the correct preposition (a, b, c, or d) that correctly completes the sentence.

1. Were you planning _____ telling the boss about the trouble we had today?
    a. in b. between c. on d. with

2. He praised me _____ my achievement.
    a. of b. for c. in d. with

3. The native people pray _____ rain with that dance.
    a. to b. with c. for d. by

4. They pray _____ several gods in that culture.
    a. to b. of c. with d. about

5. Joe said he prefers the iPhone _____ the Blackberry.
    a. on b. to c. in d. for

6. I wasn't prepared _____ her news. What a shock!
    a. for b. of c. about d. by

7. It is my pleasure to present Maria _____ this award for salesperson of the year!
    a. with b. against c. from d. on

8. The boss prevented me _____ going on that business trip.
    a. at b. from c. into d. to

9. You are prohibited _____ using your cell phone on an airplane.
    a. upon b. away c. from d. if

10. This case will protect your phone _____ damage if you drop it.
    a. from   b. between   c. in   d. with

11. This information is provided _____ educational purposes only.
    a. with   b. of   c. for   d. in

12. The copier company provides us _____ excellent service.
    a. by   b. to   c. for   d. with

No. 157: punish for

Grammar Pattern:
- **punish** [someone] **for** [something]

Preposition Focus:
- We use **for** to indicate the purpose of punishing.

Usage:
- A person or organization can **punish** another person **for** something.

Examples:
- The professor **punished** several students **for** not submitting their reports on time.
- The boss said he is going **punish** Jay **for** missing the meeting.

No. 158: quarrel about

Grammar Pattern:
- **quarrel about** [something]

Preposition Focus:
- We use **about** to indicate the topic of quarreling.

Usage:
- People can **quarrel about** something.

Examples:
- The accounting manager and his subordinate often **quarrel about** trivial things.
- Lisa and David often **quarrel about** money.

No. 159: quarrel with

Grammar Pattern:
- quarrel **with** [someone]

Preposition Focus:
- We use **with** to show the object of quarreling.

Usage:
- A person can **quarrel with** another person.

Examples:
- What happened today? I heard the boss was **quarreling with** Chuck all afternoon.
- Patty was **quarreling with** her husband about his excessive drinking.

No. 160: react to

Grammar Pattern:
- **react to** [someone]/[something]

Preposition Focus:
- We use **to** when we show the object of reacting.

Usage:
- A person can **react to** another person or thing.

Examples:
- How did the boss **react to** the news that we lost the bid?
- Brad's wife didn't **react** well **to** the news that he is being transferred to Tokyo for three months.

No. 161: recover from

Grammar Pattern:
- **recover from** [something]

Preposition Focus:
- We use **from** to indicate the source of recovering.

Usage:
- A person can **recover from** a bad or negative situation.

Examples:
- Tomoko said she is **recovering** well **from** the flu and should be back to work on Monday.
- We finally **recovered from** the downturn in sales last quarter.

No. 162: refer to

Grammar Pattern:
- **refer** [someone]/[something] **to**

Preposition Focus:
- We use **to** when we show the object of referring.

Usage:
- A person or a thing can **refer** another person or thing **to** another person or thing.

Examples:
- Our customer in Bangkok **referred** me **to** several leads there. I think we can start expanding our business there.
- If you'd like, I can **refer** you **to** a good dentist.

No. 163: relate to

Grammar Pattern:
- **relate to** [someone]/[something]

Preposition Focus:
- We use **to** when we show the object of relating.

Usage:
- A person can **relate to** another person or thing.

Examples:
- How are the sales results **related to** the marketing plan?
- The rising cost of consumer goods is **related to** the increase in oil prices.

No. 164: rely on

Grammar Pattern:
- **rely on** [someone]/[something]

Preposition Focus:
- We use **on** to show the target of **relying**.

Usage:
- A person can **rely on** another person or thing.

Examples:
- I always **rely on** Yalcin to help me when I have a computer problem.
- The boss is **relying on** us to finish this project by Friday, so let's get to work.

No. 165: remind about

Grammar Pattern:
- **remind** [someone] **about** [something]

Preposition Focus:
- We use **about** to indicate the topic of reminding.

Usage:
- A person or a thing can **remind** another person **about** something.

Examples:
- Even though I **reminded** Ted **about** the deadline several times, he turned in the report late.
- I am going to **remind** everyone **about** our sales target during the meeting.

No. 166: remind of

Grammar Pattern:
- **remind** [someone] **of** [something]

Preposition Focus:
- We use **of** to show the reason of reminding.

Usage:
- A person or a thing can **remind** another person **of** something.

Examples:
- The new sales manager **reminds** me **of** one of my college professors.
- That story **reminds** me **of** the first time I went to Osaka.

No. 167: reply to

Grammar Pattern:
- **reply to** [someone]/[something]

Preposition Focus:
- We use **to** when we show the object of replying.

Usage:
- A person can **reply to** another person or thing.

Examples:
- I couldn't **reply to** your email because I am still waiting for the answer from my boss about the matter.
- Have you **replied to** the accounting manager? He needs a response by the end of the day.

No. 168: rescue from

Grammar Pattern:
- **rescue** [someone] **from** [something]

Preposition Focus:
- We use **from** to indicate the source of rescuing.

Usage:
- A person can **rescue** another person or situation.

Examples:
- Thanks for **rescuing** me **from** talking to Jack. He tends to talk on and on.
- I was hoping someone would **rescue** me **from** the boss, but nobody helped me.

Review Quiz #14

Read the sentence and choose the correct preposition (a, b, c, or d) that correctly completes the sentence.

1. I think he was punished _____ hitting his teacher.
    a. for   b. of   c. with   d. about

2. What do you think they are quarrelling _____ now?
    a. about   b. in   c. for   d. on

3. Why does Maria quarrel _____ Glenn so much?
    a. with   b. about   c. to   d. for

4. Jack reacted badly _____ the news of the company layoff.
    a. to   b. against c. from   d. on

5. Finally, sales have recovered _____ the drop last quarter.
    a. from   b. to   c. at   d. into

6. Chuck referred me _____ a couple of guys who are interested in the marketing position.
    a. if   b. to   c. away   d. upon

7. The information in this report is related _____ the company structure and budget.
    a. in   b. between c. to   d. with

8. You can always rely _____ Frank to do a good job
    a. of   b. on   c. in   d. with

9. I had to remind Bob several times _____ the project deadline.
    a. to   b. about   c. for   d. by

10. This photo reminds me _____ my trip to Tokyo.
    a. to   b. of   c. with   d. about

11. Oh no! I forgot to reply _____ John today.
    a. on   b. to   c. in   d. for

12. When I was stranded at the train station last night, Jane came and rescued me _____ the cold.
    a. for   b. of   c. about   d. from

No. 169: resign from

Grammar Pattern:
- **resign from** [something]

Preposition Focus:
- We use **from** to indicate the source of resigning.

Usage:
- A person can **resign from** a job or a company.

Examples:
- After forty-five years in the company, Yoshi **resigned from** the board of directors.
- I have decided to **resign from** my position as marketing manager.

No. 170: respond to

Grammar Pattern:
- **respond to** [someone]/[something]

Preposition Focus:
- We use **to** when we show the object of responding.

Usage:
- A person can **respond to** another person or written correspondence (like email).

Examples:
- I have to **respond to** the sales manager by tomorrow, but I am not sure how I can get all of the information by then.
- The HR director **responded to** a variety of questions from the angry employees.

No. 171: result in

Grammar Pattern:
- **result in** [something]

Preposition Focus:
- We use **in** to show the object of resulting.

Usage:
- Something, such as a persons effort, can **result in** something.

Examples:
- All of the effort of the sales team **resulted in** a record breaking profit last quarter.
- Jack's bad attitude during the meeting **resulted in** the boss firing him.

No. 172: retire from

Grammar Pattern:
- **retire from** [something]

Preposition Focus:
- We use **from** to indicate the source of retiring.

Usage:
- A person can **retire from** a job or a company.

Examples:
- When Jay **retired from** the company, they offered him a position as a consultant.
- My uncle became a taxi driver after he **retired from** his job.

No. 173: return from

Grammar Pattern:
- **return from** [something]

Preposition Focus:
- We use **from** to indicate the source of returning.

Usage:
- A person can **return from** a place.

Examples:
- I **returned from** the training session with a better understanding of the company policy.
- I'll **return from** my trip to London on May 3rd. Let's discuss the matter at that time.

No. 174: rob of

Grammar Pattern:
- **rob** [someone] **of** [something]

Preposition Focus:
- We use **of** to show the object of robbing.

Usage:
- A person can **rob** another person or a place **of** something.

Examples:
- On the way home last night, someone **robbed** me **of** my cell phone.
- Someone **robbed** the office **of** a laptop and a camera.

No. 175: save from

Grammar Pattern:
- **save** [someone] **from** [something]

Preposition Focus:
- We use **from** to indicate the source of saving.

Usage:
- A person or something can **save** a person **from** another person or something.

Examples:
- Thanks for your help. You **saved** me **from** completing the report incorrectly.
- Jack picked up my package from the post office. That **saved** me **from** having to go there.

No. 176: scold for

Grammar Pattern:
- **scold** [someone] **for** [something]

Preposition Focus:
- We use **for** to indicate the purpose of scolding.

Usage:
- A person can **scold** another person **for** their actions.

Examples:
- The boss **scolded** me **for** missing my sales target.
- Chuck **scolded** his son **for** failing the exam.

No. 177: search for

Grammar Pattern:
- **search for** [someone]/[something]

Preposition Focus:
- We use **for** to indicate the purpose of searching.

Usage:
- A person can **search for** another person or something.

Examples:
- I'm **searching for** a different way to connect to the network. Do you know how I can do that?
- I was **searching for** new office space, but it is difficult to find exactly the perfect location.

No. 178: see about

Grammar Pattern:
- **see about** [something]

Preposition Focus:
- We use **about** to indicate the topic of seeing.

Usage:
- A person can **see about** doing something.

Examples:
- I need to **see about** renting more space for the business conference.
- We should **see about** getting new computers for the office.

No. 179: see to

Grammar Pattern:
- **see to** [something]

Preposition Focus:
- We use **to** when we show the object of seeing.

Usage:
- A person can **see to** another person or something.

Examples:
- I'm busy because I need to **see to** the new interns.
- I need to **see to** it that everyone is getting their work done on time.

No. 180: send for

Grammar Pattern:
- **send for** [someone]/[something]

Preposition Focus:
- We use **for** to indicate the purpose of sending.

Usage:
- A person can **send for** another person or something.

Examples:
- If you don't stop, I will **send for** the police.
- Can you **send for** a doctor? I think the boss is having trouble breathing.

Review Quiz #15

Read the sentence and choose the correct preposition (a, b, c, or d) that correctly completes the sentence.

1. If the CEO resigns _____ his position, he may become a board member.
    a. for   b. against   c. from   d. on

2. Why didn't you respond _____ my email?
    a. at   b. with   c. into   d. to

3. Our negotiations resulted _____ several new business deals.
    a. upon   b. away   c. if   d. in

4. I think I'm ready to retire _____ the company and move to Miami.
    a. to   b. from   c. in   d. with

5. When will Tomoko return _____ Osaka?
    a. with   b. from   c. of   d. in

6. We were robbed _____ several hundred dollars over the weekend.
    a. of   b. to   c. for   d. from

7. I can fix your PC and save you _____ having to call a technician.
    a. of   b. with   c. from   d. about

8. My wife will scold me _____ coming home so late.
    a. in   b. of   c. for   d. on

9. Are you searching _____ your keys? I saw them on the kitchen table.
    a. of   b. about   c. for   d. to

10. I have to see _____ getting some news office furniture.
    a. about   b. against   c. from   d. on

11. Please see _____ it that the supply cabinet is properly filled.
    a. for   b. to   c. at   d. into

12. I sent _____ a taxi to take us to the airport.
    a. if   b. upon   c. for   d. away

No. 181: separate from

Grammar Pattern:
- **separate** [A] **from** [B]

Preposition Focus:
- We use **from** to indicate the main [A] that [B] is separating.

Usage:
- A person can **separate from** another person, or separate something from another thing.

Examples:
- We need to **separate** the domestic customer files **from** the international customer files.
- I have to **separate** Jim **from** Greg. They waste too much time chatting with each other.

No. 182: share with

Grammar Pattern:
- **share** [something] **with** [someone]

Preposition Focus:
- We use **with** to show the person to whom the object is being shared.

Usage:
- One person can **share** something **with** another.

Examples:
- Can you share the **sales** results **with** us at the meeting tomorrow?
- I am going to **share** the good news **with** Ted as soon as I see him this afternoon.

No. 183: shout at

Grammar Pattern:
- **shout at** [someone]

Preposition Focus:
- We use **at** to indicate the target point of shouting.

Usage:
- A person can **shout at** another person.

Examples:
- Who was the boss **shouting at** this morning?
- If you weren't listening to the music so loudly, I wouldn't need to **shout at** you!

No. 184: show up at

Grammar Pattern:
- **show up at** [something]

Preposition Focus:
- We use **at** to indicate the target point of showing up.

Usage:
- A person can **show up at** a place.

Examples:
- Mark **showed up at** the meeting ten minutes late. The boss was so upset.
- Let me know when Nobi **shows up at** the office. I need to talk to her.

No. 185: smile at

Grammar Pattern:
- **smile at** [someone]

Preposition Focus:
- We use **at** to indicate the target point of smiling.

Usage:
- A person can **smile at** another person.

Examples:
- The receptionist is very nice and always **smiles at** everyone.
- Katie always **smiles at** me. I think she likes me.

No. 186: speak to

Grammar Pattern:
- **speak to** [someone]

Preposition Focus:
- We use **to** when we show the direction of speaking.

Usage:
- A person can **speak to** another person.

Examples:
- I'd like to **speak to** the manager please.
- Can I **speak to** you for a few minutes?

No. 187: speak about

Grammar Pattern:
- **speak about** [something]

Preposition Focus:
- We use **about** when we show the topic of speaking.

Usage:
- A person can **speak about** a topic.

Examples:
- The CFO is going to **speak about** the new accounting system tomorrow.
- I need to **speak** to Ted **about** the meeting time.

No. 188: specialize in

Grammar Pattern:
- **specialize in** [something]

Preposition Focus:
- We use **in** to show the object of specializing.

Usage:
- A person can **specialize in** something.

Examples:
- Nick **specializes in** graphic design and database programming.
- ABC Company **specializes in** import and export.

No. 189: spend on

Grammar Pattern:
- **spend** money **on** [someone]/[something]

Preposition Focus:
- We use **on** to show the target of spending.

Usage:
- A person can **spend** time, money, and effort **on** another person or something

Examples:
- The company **spent** a lot of money **on** advertising this quarter.
- We **spent** a lot of time **on** this project. I hope the boss likes it!

No. 190: stand for

Grammar Pattern:
- **stand for** [something]

Preposition Focus:
- We use **for** to indicate the purpose of standing.

Usage:
- Something **stands for** another thing.

Examples:
- The company logo **stands for** its solid reputation and dependablity.
- This symbol **stands for** our company's long history and success.

No. 191: stare at

Grammar Pattern:
- **stare at** [someone]/[something]

Preposition Focus:
- We use **at** to indicate the target point of staring.

Usage:
- A person can **stare at** another person or something.

Examples:
- My eyes are tired because I have been **staring at** the computer screen all day.
- Why do you keep **staring at** me. Is there something wrong?

No. 192: stem from

Grammar Pattern:
- **stem from** [someone]/[something]

Preposition Focus:
- We use **from** to indicate the source of stemming.

Usage:
- Something **stems from** another thing.

Examples:
- The network problem **stems from** a defective router. If we replace the router, the problem should go away.
- The problems you are having with your staff **stem from** inadequate training.

Review Quiz #16

Read the sentence and choose the correct preposition (a, b, c, or d) that correctly completes the sentence.

1. Starting in December, we have to separate glass, plastic, and paper _____ the rest of the trash. It's for the new recycling program.
    a. from   b. between   c. in   d. with

2. I want to share some interesting news _____ you.
    a. of   b. with   c. in   d. to

3. Why are you shouting _____ me? I didn't do anything wrong.
    a. to   b. for   c. at   d. by

4. I heard that Chuck showed _____ late again this morning.
    a. at   b. of   c. with   d. up

5. I love it when you smile _____ me.
    a. on   b. at   c. in   d. for

6. I spoke _____ several customers at the trade show.
    a. for   b. of   c. about   d. to

7. Hi. This is Mike. Can I speak _____ the IT manager please?
    a. with   b. against   c. from   d. on

8. What sort of products does your company specialize _____?
    a. at   b. in   c. into   d. to

9. We've spent too much money _____ that computer system.
    a. upon   b. away   c. on   d. if

10. The acronym BTW stands _____ "by the way."
    a. for   b. between   c. in   d. with

11. A strange guy stared _____ me on the subway this morning.
    a. with   b. at   c. of   d. in

12. Her problems stem _____ her lack of effort and enthusiasm.
    a. by   b. to   c. for   d. from

No. 193: stop from

Grammar Pattern:
- **stop** [someone] **from** [something]

Preposition Focus:
- We use **from** to indicate the source of stopping.

Usage:
- A person can **stop** another person **from** doing something.

Examples:
- The landlord tried to **stop** us **from** remodeling the conference room.
- The rain **stopped** me **from** playing golf today.

No. 194: subject to

Grammar Pattern:
- **subject** [someone] **to** [something]

Preposition Focus:
- We use **to** when we show the object of subjecting.

Usage:
- A person or something can **subject** a person **to** another person or something.

Examples:
- This project has **subjected** everyone **to** a lot of overtime.
- The boss **subjected** us **to** a two hour speech about improving sales.

No. 195: subscribe to

Grammar Pattern:
- **subscribe to** [something]

Preposition Focus:
- We use **to** when we show the object of subscribing.

Usage:
- A person can **subscribe to** something like a magazine or website.

Examples:
- We **subscribe to** several magazines.
- Some parts of that website are free, but you need to **subscribe to** it if you want to see the videos.

No. 196: substitute for

Grammar Pattern:
- **substitute** [A] **for** [B]

Preposition Focus:
- We use **for** to indicate the [B] that [A] is substituted for.

Usage:
- A person or something can **substitute for** another person or something.

Examples:
- On the website you can **substitute** the photo of the CEO **for** the photo of the chairman.
- Ted has to leave the office now, so I will **substitute for** him at the meeting.

No. 197: subtract from

Grammar Pattern:
- **subtract** [something] **from** [something]

Preposition Focus:
- We use **from** to indicate the source of subtracting.

Usage:
- A person can **subtract** something **from** another thing.

Examples:
- If you **subtract** ten **from** seventy, you get sixty.
- Jane has a lot of energy. Nothing can **subtract from** her work ethic.

No. 198: succeed at

Grammar Pattern:
- **succeed at** [something]

Preposition Focus:
- We use **at** to indicate the target point of succeeding.

Usage:
- A person can **succeed at** doing something.

Examples:
- I finally **succeeded at** getting the boss to approve of my vacation.
- Good luck on your trip to Dubai. I hope you **succeed at** winning the contract.

No. 199: succeed in

Grammar Pattern:
- **succeed in** [something]

Preposition Focus:
- We use **in** to show the object of succeeding.

Usage:
- A person can **succeed in** doing something.

Examples:
- I **succeeded in** convincing the boss to let me take a vacation.
- I'm trying to **succeed in** learning the new database system, but it is difficult.

No. 200: suffer from

Grammar Pattern:
- **suffer from** [something]

Preposition Focus:
- We use **from** to indicate the source of suffering.

Usage:
- A person can **suffer from** something, like a sickness.

Examples:
- Andy is **suffering from** the flu, so he'll be out of the office all week.
- This quarter, we are **suffering from** a lack of sales.

No. 201: suspect of

Grammar Pattern:
- **suspect** [someone] **of** [something]

Preposition Focus:
- We use **of** to show the reason for suspecting.

Usage:
- A person can **suspect** another person **of** doing something.

Examples:
- The boss **suspected** Chuck **of** taking the missing iPad.
- Eddie called out sick again, but the manager **suspects** him **of** lying.

No. 202: talk about

Grammar Pattern:
- **talk about** [someone]/[something]

Preposition Focus:
- We use **about** to indicate the topic of talking.

Usage:
- A person can **talk about** another person or something.

Examples:
- We were **talking about** the company picnic.
- What do you want to **talk** to me **about**?

No. 203: talk to

Grammar Pattern:
- **talk to** [someone]

Preposition Focus:
- We use **to** when we show the direction of talking.

Usage:
- A person can **talk to** another person.

Examples:
- I need to **talk to** the boss about the sales meeting.
- I **talked to** three people in customer service, but nobody could help me.

No. 204: talk with

Grammar Pattern:
- **talk with** [someone]

Preposition Focus:
- We use **with** when we show the direction of talking.

Usage:
- A person can talk **with** another person.

Examples:
- I was **talking with** Jenny today. I think she likes you!
- We should **talk with** the boss before working on this project.

Review Quiz #17

Read the sentence and choose the correct preposition (a, b, c, or d) that correctly completes the sentence.

1. You can't stop me _____ going there. I've already booked the flight.
    a. from   b. of   c. with   d. about

2. We were subjected _____ an additional security check at the airport.
    a. in   b. to   c. for   d. on

3. Which magazines and newspapers do you subscribe _____?
    a. of   b. about   c. to   d. for

4. This coffee creamer is a good substitute _____ milk.
    a. for   b. against   c. from   d. on

5. Once you subtract the expenses _____ the revenue, you are left with the profit.
    a. to   b. at   c. from   d. into

6. Were you able to succeed _____ getting the boss to give you a raise?
    a. at   b. for   c. away   d. to

7. I think Sam succeeded _____ passing all of his final exams.
    a. for   b. between   c. in   d. with

8. This spring, a lot of people suffered _____ allergies.
    a. of   b. from   c. in   d. with

9. She suspected me _____ cheating, but I was just taking dance lessons after work.
    a. of   b. for   c. to   d. by

10. What did you talk _____ during the meeting?
    a. about   b. of   c. with   d. to

11. Let me know if you want to talk _____ me about my trip.
    a. on   b. to   c. in   d. for

12. I haven't talked _____ Jane for a long time. How is she?
    a. for   b. of   c. about   d. with

No. 205: tell about

Grammar Pattern:
- **tell** [someone] **about** [something]

Preposition Focus:
- We use **about** to indicate the topic of telling.

Usage:
- A person can **tell** another person **about** something.

Examples:
- Can you **tell** me more **about** the conference?
- Sam **told** me **about** the conference. He said it was pretty interesting.

No. 206: thank for

Grammar Pattern:
- **thank** [someone] **for** [something]

Preposition Focus:
- We use **for** to indicate the purpose of thanking.

Usage:
- A person can **thank** another person **for** something.

Examples:
- I really want to **thank** you **for** helping me yesterday. How about having dinner tomorrow?
- He gave me this bottle of wine to **thank** me **for** helping him.

No. 207: think about

Grammar Pattern:
- **think about** [someone]/[something]

Preposition Focus:
- We use **about** to indicate the topic of thinking.

Usage:
- A person can **think about** another person or something.

Examples:
- We are **thinking about** opening a branch office in Mexico City.
- I'm **thinking about** pizza for lunch. How about you?

No. 208: think of

Grammar Pattern:
- **think of** [someone]/[something]

Preposition Focus:
- We use **of** to show the object of thinking.

Usage:
- A person can **think of** another person or something.

Examples:
- We need to **think of** a way to expand our operations in Asia.
- I can't **think of** a better person for the sales job than Lori.

No. 209: translate from/into

Grammar Pattern:
- **translate** [something] **from** [something]

Preposition Focus:
- We use **from** to indicate the source of translating. We use **into** to indicate the result of translating

Usage:
- A person can **translate** something **from** one language **into** another.

Examples:
- I need to have this document **translated from** Japanese **into** English.
- Can you **translate** this memo **into** Spanish?

No. 210: travel to

Grammar Pattern:
- **travel to** [somewhere]

Preposition Focus:
- We use **to** when we show the direction of traveling

Usage:
- A person can **travel to** a place.

Examples:
- I can't have dinner tomorrow because I have to **travel to** Boston right after the meeting.
- I **travel to** work by train every morning.

No. 211: turn to

Grammar Pattern:
- **turn to** [someone]

Preposition Focus:
- We use **to** when we show the direction or object of turning.

Usage:
- A person can **turn to** another person.

Examples:
- I was surprised when Jane **turned to** me and handed me the award.
- When he **turned to** me I smiled and said thanks.

No. 212: use for

Grammar Pattern:
- **use** [something] **for** [something]

Preposition Focus:
- We use **for** to indicate the purpose of using.

Usage:
- A person can **use** something **for** some purpose.

Examples:
- You can **use** this external hard drive **for** any computer, MAC or Windows.
- What do you **use** this laptop **for**?

No. 213: vote for

Grammar Pattern:
- **vote for** [someone]/[something]

Preposition Focus:
- We use **for** to indicate the target of voting.

Usage:
- A person can **vote for** another person or thing.

Examples:
- The board of directors **voted for** Serena to be the next CFO.
- I **vote for** going home early today. Is anybody with me?

No. 214: vouch for

Grammar Pattern:
- **vouch for** [someone]

Preposition Focus:
- We use **for** to indicate the purpose of vouching.

Usage:
- A person can **vouch for** another person.

Examples:
- I can **vouch for** Chuck. He is the best salesman in the company.
- Andy, please **vouch for** me. Tell her how reliable I am.

No. 215: wait for

Grammar Pattern:
- **wait** [someone] **for** [something]

Preposition Focus:
- We use **for** to indicate the purpose of waiting.

Usage:
- A person can **wait for** another person or thing.

Examples:
- Can you **wait for** me to finish this report? It will only take another thirty minutes.
- Finally my new laptop came. I've **waited** a week **for** it.

No. 216: walk into

Grammar Pattern:
- **walk into** [something]

Preposition Focus:
- We use **into** to show the destination of walking

Usage:
- A person can **walk into** a place (like a room) or an object.

Examples:
- Everyone stood up when Jim **walked into** the room.
- I **walked into** the store and saw my sister.

Review Quiz #18

Read the sentence and choose the correct preposition (a, b, c, or d) that correctly completes the sentence.

1. Why didn't you tell me _____ the accident?
    a. on	b. against	c. from	d. about

2. Thank you so much _____ your assistance last week. I appreciate it.
    a. at	b. for	c. into	d. to

3. I'm thinking _____ going to San Diego for the weekend. Would you like to join me?
    a. upon	b. away	c. about	d. if

4. I can't think _____ any reason why the boss wouldn't agree with your ideas.
    a. of	b. between	c. in	d. with

5. We've translated our catalog _____ English _____ several languages.
    a. with/into	b. from/into	c. of/into	d. in/into

6. I heard that Andy is traveling _____ Tokyo for the first time.
    a. by	b. at	c. for	d. to

7. She turned _____ me and handed me the envelope.
    a. to	b. of	c. with	d. about

8. Jane uses this book _____ improving her English!
    a. in	b. for	c. of	d. on

9. Nick said he has voted _____ the same political party all his life.
    a. of	b. about	c. for	d. in

10. Can you vouch _____ me? I think the boss doesn't believe me.
    a. for	b. against	c. from	d. on

11. I've been waiting _____ the bus for almost a half hour. I wonder what happened.
    a. to	b. for	c. at	d. into

12. When Greg walked _____ the house we shouted "happy birthday!"
    a. for	b. on	c. of	d. into

No. 217: warn about

Grammar Pattern:
- **warn** [someone] **about** [something]

Preposition Focus:
- We use **about** to indicate the topic of warning.

Usage:
- A person can **warn** another person **about** something.

Examples:
- The accounting manager **warned** Mike **about** keeping the receipts from his business trips.
- I've **warned** you **about** coming to work late several times. If it happens again, you're fired.

No. 218: warn against

Grammar Pattern:
- **warn** [someone] **against** [something]

Preposition Focus:
- We use **against** to indicate the opposition to warning.

Usage:
- A person can **warn** another person **against** doing something.

Examples:
- He warned me against going to that trade show and he was right. It was not so busy at all.
- I **warned** him **against** coming to the office late.

No. 219: waste on

Grammar Pattern:
- **waste** time/money/effort **on** [someone]/[something]

Preposition Focus:
- We use **on** to show the target of wasting.

Usage:
- A person can **waste** time, money, and effort **on** another person or something

Examples:
- If you think the boss is not going to approve this proposal, I'm going to stop working on it. I don't want to **waste** my time **on** something for nothing.
- I **wasted** an hour **on** that customer. He didn't buy anything!

No. 220: wish for

Grammar Pattern:
- **wish for** [something]

Preposition Focus:
- We use **for** to indicate the purpose of wishing.

Usage:
- A person can **wish for** something.

Examples:
- I'm **wishing for** a better result next year.
- Be careful about what you **wish for**. You may just get it!

No. 221: wonder about

Grammar Pattern:
- **wonder about** [someone]/[something]

Preposition Focus:
- We use **about** to indicate the topic of wondering.

Usage:
- A person can **wonder about** something.

Examples:
- I was **wondering about** the meeting. How did it go?
- The boss is **wondering about** who he can send to Denver next month.

No. 222: work for

Grammar Pattern:
- **work for** [company/person]

Preposition Focus:
- We use **for** to show the relationship of working.

Usage:
- A person can **work for** a company or **work for** another person.

Examples:
- I've been **working for** ABC company since 2005.
- Harry used to **work for** Bob Jones at BVC Bank.

No. 223: work in

Grammar Pattern:
- **work in** [business field]

Preposition Focus:
- We use **in** to show the related field of work

Usage:
- A person can **work in** an industry or business field.

Examples:
- Jackie **works in** medical equipment sales.
- I **worked in** the music business for 14 years before becoming an English teacher.

No. 224: work on

Grammar Pattern:
- **work on** [someone]/[something]

Preposition Focus:
- We use **on** to show the target of working

Usage:
- A person can **work on** something.

Examples:
- We need to start **working on** next year's budget.
- Can you **work on** the website updates with me?

No. 225: work with

Grammar Pattern:
- **work with** [someone]/[something]

Preposition Focus:
- We use **with to** show the people working together.

Usage:
- A person can **work with** another person or a team.

Examples:
- I have been **working with** this team for 2 years. It's been a great experience!
- I worked **with** Nobuko for ten years. She's just fabulous.

No. 226: worry about

Grammar Pattern:
- **worry about** [someone]/[something]

Preposition Focus:
- We use **about** to indicate the topic of worrying.

Usage:
- A person can **worry about** another person or thing.

Examples:
- I'm **worried about** Ted. His sales have been falling recently.
- You don't need to **worry about** the trade show. Dee and I will take care of everything.

No. 227: write about

Grammar Pattern:
- **write about** [someone]/[something]

Preposition Focus:
- We use **about** to indicate the topic of writing.

Usage:
- A person can **write about** a topic.

Examples:
- I heard from Yumi yesterday. She **wrote about** her experience at the trade show.
- Adam **writes about** marketing in several trade publications.

No. 228: write to

Grammar Pattern:
- **write to** [someone]

Preposition Focus:
- We use **to** when we show the object of writing.

Usage:
- A person can **write to** another person or an organization.

Examples:
- I **wrote to** the shipping company several times, but they haven't replied yet. I wonder why.
- **Write to** me when you get to Milan and let me know how the trip is going.

Review Quiz #19

Read the sentence and choose the correct preposition (a, b, c, or d) that correctly completes the sentence.

1. I tried to warn her _____ that guy, but she didn't want to hear it.
    a. about   b. away   c. if   d. upon

2. We were warned _____ driving in the snow.
    a. between   b. against   c. in   d. with

3. Why did I waste my time _____ that report? I don't think he read it.
    a. with   b. on   c. of   d. in

4. Blow out the candles and wish _____ something nice for your birthday.
    a. at   b. for   c. by   d. to

5. Do you sometimes wonder _____ our friends from high school?
    a. for   b. about   c. of   d. with

6. In my country, most people work _____ the same company their entire life.
    a. of   b. to   c. from   d. for

7. Ted decided that he want's to work _____ insurance after graduation.
    a. in   b. of   c. for   d. to

8. Did you start working _____ the ABC project?
    a. about   b. of   c. for   d. on

9. It's such a pleasure to work _____ all of you.
    a. on   b. against   c. with   d. from

10. I'm not worried _____ giving the presentation. I've done it several times.
 a. to b. at c. into d. about

11. Dick wrote _____ his experience in Dubai on his blog.
 a. upon b. about c. away d. if

12. I wrote _____ them this morning. Hopefully they will get back to me by the end of the day.
 a. to b. with c. between d. at

Quiz Answer Key

	RQ 1	RQ 2	RQ 3	RQ 4	RQ 5	RQ 6	RQ 7	RQ 8	RQ 9	RQ 10
1	A	A	B	D	D	C	A	A	B	A
2	B	D	B	C	C	B	B	B	D	B
3	C	B	A	C	C	C	C	D	D	C
4	A	D	A	A	A	C	A	A	B	D
5	B	D	C	B	A	B	B	B	A	D
6	D	A	D	C	D	B	B	D	C	D
7	D	C	B	A	A	A	B	C	D	A
8	B	C	D	B	B	B	B	B	C	B
9	A	C	D	D	D	C	C	C	B	C
10	A	A	C	C	A	A	A	A	B	B
11	B	C	C	A	B	B	B	B	A	D
12	D	B	A	D	D	B	C	D	A	D

	RQ 11	RQ 12	RQ 13	RQ 14	RQ 15	RQ 16	RQ 17	RQ 18	RQ 19
1	A	A	C	A	C	A	A	D	A
2	B	B	B	A	D	B	B	B	B
3	C	D	C	A	D	C	C	C	B
4	A	A	A	A	B	D	A	A	B
5	D	B	B	A	B	B	C	B	B
6	D	C	A	B	A	D	A	D	D
7	A	A	A	C	C	A	C	A	A
8	D	B	B	B	C	B	B	B	D
9	B	C	C	B	C	C	A	C	C
10	A	A	A	B	A	A	A	A	D
11	B	A	C	B	B	B	B	B	B
12	A	A	D	D	C	D	D	D	A

Index Reference

Verb & Preposition Combinations Using About

argue **about (15)**
ask **about (18)**
boast **about (28)**
care **about (30)**
communicate **about (37)**
complain **about (43)**
dream **about (75)**
feel **about (92)**
forget **about (97)**
grumble **about (101)**
hear **about (104)**
joke **about (121)**
know **about (125)**
laugh **about (126)**
learn **about (128)**
quarrel **about (158)**
remind **about (165)**
see **about (178)**
speak **about (187)**
talk **about (202)**
tell **about (205)**
think **about (207)**
warn **about (217)**
wonder **about (221)**
worry **about (226)**
write **about (227)**

Verb & Preposition Combinations Using Against

decide against **(60)**
fight against **(94)**
insure against **(113)**
warn against **(218)**

Verb & Preposition Combinations Using At

guess at **(102)**
laugh at **(127)**

look at **(135)**
shout at **(183)**
show up at **(184)**
smile at **(185)**
stare at **(191)**
succeed at **(198)**

Verb & Preposition Combinations Using Between

choose **between (33)**
decide **between (61)**

Verb & Preposition Combinations Using For

account **for (1)**
admire **for (6)**
apologize **for (10)**
apply **for (12)**
arrange **for (17)**
ask **for (19)**
beg **for (22)**
blame **for (27)**
care **for (31)**
congratulate **for (49)**
exchange **for (83)**
excuse **for (85)**
fight **for (95)**
forgive **for (98)**
hope **for (110)**
invite **for (118)**
keep **for (123)**
leave **for (129)**
listen **for (132)**
long **for (134)**
look **for (136)**
mistake **for (139)**
pay **for (143)**
praise **for (146)**
pray **for (147)**
prepare **for (150)**
provide **for (155)**

punish **for** **(157)**
scold **for** **(176)**
search **for** **(177)**
send **for** **(180)**
stand **for** **(190)**
substitute **for** **(196)**
thank **for** **(206)**
use **for** **(212)**
vote **for** **(213)**
vouch **for** **(214)**
wait **for** **(215)**
wish **for** **(220)**
work **for** **(222)**
feel **for** **(93)**

Verb & Preposition Combinations Using From

benefit **from** **(26)**
borrow **from** **(29)**
come **from** **(35)**
demand **from** **(63)**
derive **from** **(65)**
deter **from** **(66)**
differ **from** **(68)**
discourage **from** **(71)**
distinguish **from** **(73)**
distract **from** **(74)**
emerge **from** **(81)**
escape **from** **(82)**
exclude **from** **(84)**
excuse **from** **(86)**
expel **from** **(87)**
graduate **from** **(100)**
hear **from** **(105)**
hide **from** **(108)**
hinder **from** **(109)**
keep away **from** **(124)**
leave **from** **(130)**
prevent **from** **(152)**
prohibit **from** **(153)**

protect **from (154)**
recover **from (161)**
rescue **from (168)**
resign **from (169)**
retire **from (172)**
return **from (173)**
save **from (175)**
separate **from (181)**
stem **from (192)**
stop **from (193)**
subtract **from (197)**
suffer **from (200)**
translate from/into **(209)**

Verb & Preposition Combinations Using In
believe **in (24)**
compete **in (41)**
dress **in (77)**
dress **in (78)**
interfere **in (114)**
invest **in (117)**
involve **in (120)**
participate **in (142)**
persist **in (144)**
result **in (171)**
specialize **in (188)**
succeed **in (199)**
work **in (223)**

Verb & Preposition Combinations Using Into
crash into **(58)**
translate from/into **(209)**
walk into **(216)**

Verb & Preposition Combinations Using Of
accuse **of (2)**
approve **of (14)**
become **of (21)**
consist **of (52)**

convince **of (54)**
cure **of (59)**
disapprove **of (70)**
dream **of (76)**
hear **of (106)**
remind **of (166)**
rob **of (174)**
suspect **of (201)**
think **of (208)**

Verb & Preposition Combinations Using On

agree **on (8)**
base **on (20)**
comment **on (36)**
compliment **on (45)**
concentrate **on (46)**
congratulate **on (50)**
decide **on (62)**
elaborate **on (80)**
experiment **on (88)**
impress **on (111)**
insist **on (112)**
plan **on (145)**
rely **on (164)**
spend **on (189)**
waste **on (219)**
work **on (224)**
depend on/for **(64)**

Verb & Preposition Combinations Using To

adapt **to (3)**
add **to (4)**
adjust **to (5)**
admit **to (7)**
apologize **to (11)**
apply **to (13)**
belong **to (25)**
compare **to (39)**
complain **to (44)**

confess **to** (47)
consent **to** (51)
contribute **to** (53)
devote **to** (67)
drink **to** (79)
explain **to** (90)
get married **to** (99)
happen **to** (103)
introduce **to** (116)
invite **to** (119)
lend **to** (131)
listen **to** (133)
matter **to** (137)
object **to** (140)
pray **to** (148)
prefer **to** (149)
react **to** (160)
refer **to** (162)
relate **to** (163)
reply **to** (167)
respond **to** (170)
see **to** (179)
speak **to** (186)
subject **to** (194)
subscribe **to** (195)
talk **to** (203)
travel **to** (210)
turn **to** (211)
write **to** (228)

Verb & Preposition Combinations Using With

agree **with** (9)
argue **with** (16)
begin **with** (23)
charge **with** (32)
collide **with** (34)
communicate **with** (38)
compare **with** (40)
compete **with** (42)

confuse **with** **(48)**
cope **with** **(55)**
correspond **with** **(56)**
cover **with** **(57)**
disagree **with** **(69)**
discuss **with** **(72)**
experiment **with** **(89)**
face **with** **(91)**
fight **with** **(96)**
help **with** **(107)**
interfere **with** **(115)**
joke **with** **(122)**
meet **with** **(138)**
operate **with** **(141)**
present **with** **(151)**
provide **with** **(156)**
quarrel **with** **(159)**
share **with** **(182)**
talk **with** **(204)**
work **with** **(225)**

Congratulations! You've reached the end of the book and have probably discovered I've actually put 228 Combinations here! I hope you enjoyed my surprise. Thanks again for studying with me ☺

FREE Mp3 Audio Program.

Email proof of purchase of this book to me (learn@myhappyenglish.com) and I'll send you the 228 Mp3 file audio program absolutely free!

Other paperbacks & eBooks by Michael DiGiacomo

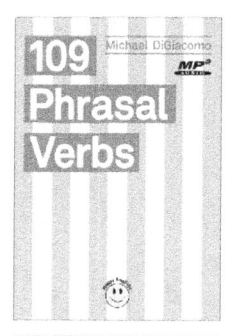

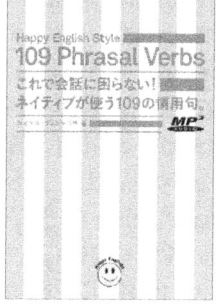

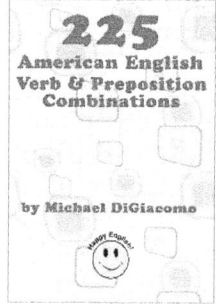

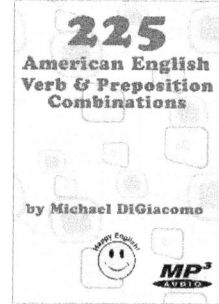

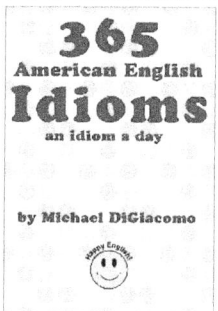

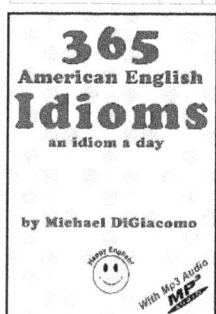

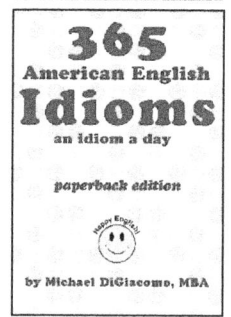

Made in the USA
Monee, IL
07 May 2020